SHIP OF FATE

The Story of the MV *Wilhelm Gustloff*

Roger Moorhouse

First published 2016 by Endeavour Press Ltd.

This edition published 2018 by Sharpe Books.

For Heinz Schön

(1926-2013)

Table of Contents

Introduction 9

Ship of Fate 14

Acknowledgements 179

Author's Note 181

Introduction

On November 10th 1943, a Paris cinema was given the dubious honour of hosting the premiere of a major German propaganda film. *Titanic* was an epic tale of English greed, stubbornness and stupidity on the high seas, which – predictably perhaps – retold the story of the ship's sinking in 1912 as a political morality tale with a blatantly anti-UK message.

It had certainly been an ambitious film, with nine huge sets built at the Babelsberg Film Studio in Berlin, as well as a 20ft replica of the vessel and the requisition of a German luxury liner – the *Cap Arcona* – to serve as a stand-in for the doomed ship for the high-seas, exterior footage. In addition, propaganda minister Joseph Goebbels had hired one of the rising stars of the German film industry; Herbert Selpin.

The director had scored a success the previous year with his anti-British film, *Carl Peters*. All of this, naturally, came at a cost; *Titanic* was allocated a record budget of 4 million RM: 12 times what some of its rival productions received.[1] Goebbels' intention was that his studio would rival Hollywood.

Unsurprisingly perhaps, *Titanic* endured a challenging production. Rumours of wild parties and illicit liaisons aboard the *Cap Arcona*, involving the ship's crew and young female extras had swirled for months, and had reached the ears of the Propaganda Ministry in Berlin.[2] In addition, the film had run beyond

---

[1] See "Nazi Titanic", Blink Films/Channel 5/History Channel documentary, 2012.

[2] Bundesarchiv, Berlin, R109II/45, Reichspropagandaamt Danzig correspondence. With thanks to Bill Niven.

schedule and way over budget, and its final version was destroyed in an RAF air raid, thereby requiring an additional period in the edit suite. To cap it all, the film's director, Selpin, had been found in his Berlin prison cell the previous summer, having apparently committed suicide after hanging himself with his braces. His death followed a rather indiscrete altercation with the film's pro-Nazi screenwriter, Walter Zerlett-Olfenius, in which he had openly and scornfully cast doubt on Germany's ability to win the war. Selpin had been denounced and arrested. Goebbels, as expected, was unsympathetic, and made only a lapidary note in his diary: "Selpin has killed himself in his cell. He has drawn the consequences that would most likely have been drawn by the state."[3] Though suicide was

---

[3] Elke Fröhlich (ed.), *Die Tagebücher von Joseph Goebbels*,

officially registered as the cause of Selpin's death, the Berlin rumour mill suggested that he had been murdered by the SS.[4]

Most seriously, however, Goebbels was also displeased with the end product. The official explanation was that he doubted the German public had the stomach for a film portrayal of panic and mass death, given they and their loved ones were themselves facing mortal danger. In his diary, he noted merely that the directing was not what it might have been – clearly unable to resist taking a posthumous swipe at Selpin – and added that he disliked the ending.[5] But it may also be that a more complex motive was at play and that the film's implicit message – criticising the blind

---

Part II, Vol. V, (Munich, 1995), p. 228.

[4] See Jared Poley, "Analysis of a Nazi *Titanic*" in *New German Review*, 17 (2001/2), pp. 7-27.

[5] Fröhlich (ed.), op. cit., Part II, Vol. VI, (Munich, 1996), p. 462.

obedience, arrogance and stupidity of the *Titanic*'s crew – was deemed too close to home. Whatever the reason, the premiere was to be held in Paris and the film would never be aired in Hitler's Reich.

The audience of German officials, honoured Parisian guests and off-duty soldiers that attended the premiere doubtless enjoyed the film, revelling in the sumptuous visual feast, soaking up the propagandist message. They were entertained, they were thrilled, certainly, but they were also being indoctrinated, just as Goebbels wanted. A few of them might have already suspected that – like the ship on the screen before them – Hitler's Reich was rushing headlong towards disaster. But, none of them could have imagined that within little over a year, Nazi Germany would have a *Titanic* of its own.

Ship of Fate

Hitler's real-life *Titanic* began its life when it slid stern-first down the slipway at the famed Blohm & Voss shipyard in Hamburg, on May 5th 1937. It was to be a vessel whose fate over the following eight years would mirror – almost exactly – that of the state in which it was born.

It was certainly an impressive sight. Perched on the slipway, towering above a mass of cheering crowds and surrounded by fluttering swastika flags. The ship measured over 200 metres from stem to stern and displaced over 25,000 tonnes, thereby larger and considerably heavier than Hitler's so-called 'pocket battleships'; the *Deutschland*, the *Admiral Scheer* and the *Graf Spee*. It was no battleship however. It was a cruise liner, one of the largest of the German commercial fleet and the first to be explicitly commissioned by the Nazis for non-military purposes.

The Nazi authorities had assiduously promoted the ship, even before it was launched. Its first rivet had been ceremonially struck a year earlier by the Head of the Reich Labour Front, Robert Ley, and a detailed scale model of the vessel had toured the country to generate public interest and enthusiasm.[6] Invitations to the launch, sent out the month before, had coyly avoided giving the vessel a name and speculation was rife that Hitler would name her after himself. Given it was a high profile event, it was natural that the Führer would be present at the launch. Standing alongside Himmler and the other

---

[6] Heinz Schön, *Hitler's Traumschiffe*, (Kiel, 2000), p. 126.

dignitaries on a raised platform beneath the ship's looming bow- He did not reach for the microphone, however. He stood as an honoured guest to hear speeches by, amongst others, the Hamburg Gauleiter; Karl Kaufmann, and the director of the shipyard, Rudolf Blohm. Finally, Robert Ley brought proceedings to a climax. Resplendent in his brown party uniform and gold braid, and manfully mastering his stutter, Ley gave forth. The ship, he proclaimed, was unique: "The first time in history that a state had undertaken to build such a large vessel for its workers. We Germans do not use any old crate for our working men and women." He added, "Only the best is good enough".[7] Rising to his task, Ley finally revealed the name that the ship was to bear: "We want every German to be strong and

[7] Ibid., p. 31.

healthy, so that Germany will live and be eternal. Thus we christen this ship with the name of one of our heroes: Wilhelm Gustloff, a man who died for Germany!"[8] With that, a name plate in Gothic script flapped into place on the ship's bow, doubtless to the bemusement of some of the estimated 50,000 present.[9]

Wilhelm Gustloff was, perhaps, a peculiar choice. Somewhat peripheral to Hitler's movement, he was the German-born leader of the Nazi Party in Switzerland, and had – since Hitler's rise to power in 1933 – expanded the party's activities there, gaining over 5,000 members from among the émigré German community and establishing 14 regional branches complete with a Hitler Youth wing.

[8] Ibid., p. 32.
[9] For accounts of the launch, see *Völkischer Beobachter*, 6 May 1937, p. 1 or *The Times*, 6 May 1937, p. 15.

Notwithstanding such efforts, Gustloff would doubtless have languished in obscurity were it not for the fact that he was assassinated in 1936. The circumstances of his death – gunned down in cold blood by a Jewish assassin – made him very useful to the Nazis for propaganda purposes. He was proclaimed as a '*Blutzeuge*'; a 'martyr' for the Nazi cause, and given a state funeral in Germany, with Hitler, Göring, Himmler and Ribbentrop all in attendance. In addition, it was decided that the cruise liner then taking shape in Hamburg would bear his name; the most famous vessel in Nazi Germany was to be named after a comparative unknown.

So it was, that it was formally christened by its namesake's widow – Hedwig Gustloff – who, standing alongside Hitler and Ley and dressed theatrically in her widow's weeds, delivered her line in a slightly strained voice, before smashing the customary bottle of champagne across the bow. With that, the huge crowd gave a ripple of applause and raised their right arms as one, while the vessel slid slowly back into the choppy waters of the Elbe estuary. The *Wilhelm Gustloff* was born.

The concept behind the *Wilhelm Gustloff* was that of state-organised leisure. Taking its cue from the analogous body in Fascist Italy – *Dopolavoro* – the Third Reich's leisure organisation was called '*Kraft durch Freude*', (meaning 'Strength through Joy') and popularly known as the KdF. Established in 1933, as a subdivision of the DAF; the German Labour Front, it had a simple premise. As Nazism itself sought to woo the ordinary German worker away from socialism towards 'National Socialism', the KdF formed an essential part of the seduction; promising holidays, cultural enrichment and sporting activities as part of the appeal. In essence, it was offering cruises and concerts in place of collective bargaining and class struggle.

Though profoundly political in intent, the KdF was not an entirely cynical exercise. Indeed, it was an expression of the socialist impulse that was part of the Nazi ethos. While Nazism is rightly remembered – and reviled – for its obsession with Aryan racial purity and its genocidal anti-Semitism, it is often forgotten that its origins lay in an attempt to provide a nationalist narrative with enough socialist content that it would appeal to ordinary Germans. This fusion of ideas is clearly evident in the Nazi Party's early manifesto: the "25 Point Programme" of 1920, in which socialist staples such as equality, nationalisation of industry, land reform and the abolition of unearned income were juxtaposed with the more conventional demands of the radical right, such as the exclusion of Jews and the political union of all members of the nation.[10]

This socialist component to Nazism's DNA was certainly diluted in the years that followed; accommodations were made with 'big business' and a cruder *realpolitik* supplanted some of the early working class populism, but it was never extinguished entirely. Indeed, Adolf Hitler was still declaring his allegiance to what he understood as 'socialism' during the 1932 election:

"I am a socialist because it seems to me incomprehensible, to maintain and treat a

---

[10] '25 Point Programme' quoted in J. Noakes & G. Pridham (eds), *Nazism 1919-1945*, Vol. 1, (Exeter, 1983), pp. 14-16.

machine with care but to leave the finest representatives of the labour, the humans themselves, to waste away. Because I want my people to climb up again one day to a high standard of living, I wish for a general increase in its performance, and therefore I stand for the men and women who accomplish these things."[11]

The KdF, therefore, should be understood in this light: as a part of that socialist element of 'National Socialism', which would be expressed in Nazi Germany via the concept of the *Volksgemeinschaft* – the idea that all Germans were members of a 'national community' that transcended class or regional divides. As its own officials proclaimed, the KdF was to serve as a "cultural tutor", teaching

---

[11] NSDAP Wahlprogramm, April 1932.

all Germans to become part of the nation; to "feel the pulse of their own blood".[12]

Of course there were other motivations at play; not least among them the crude buying of the workers' allegiance and the totalitarian desire to infiltrate and control every aspect of the individual's life. There was also an important economic rationale; that of maximising production by fostering the creation of a contented and, above all, motivated workforce.[13] "We do not send our workers to holiday on cruise ships, or build them enormous seaside resorts just for the sake of it", one KdF report explained in 1940, "We do it only to maintain and strengthen the labour potential of the individual, and to allow him to

---

[12] *Organisation der Deutschen Arbeitsfront under der NS-Gemeinschaft Kraft durch Freude*, (Berlin, 1934), pp. 24-5.
[13] Shelley Baranowski, *Strength through Joy*, (Cambridge, 2004), p. 41.

return to his workplace with renewed focus."[14] Moreover, as Hitler made clear to Robert Ley, an important motive behind the KdF was to ensure that German workers were tempered, militarised, ready for any eventuality, even war. "Make sure for me", he said, "that the people hold their nerve, for only with a people with strong nerves can we pursue politics."[15]

Clearly then, the KdF and the *Volksgemeinschaft* were not afterthoughts, they were not simply eyewash to seduce the gullible; they were an integral part of Nazi Germany's vision for its new society. Every German worker was encouraged to become a member and by 1939 over 25 million of them

---

[14] Quoted in Jürgen Rostock & Franz Zadnicek, *Paradiesruinen: Das KdF Seebad der Zwanzigtausend auf Rügen*, (Berlin, 1995), p. 24.
[15] Hitler to Robert Ley, quoted in Volker Dahm, Albert A Feiber, Hartmut Mehringer and Horst Möller (eds), *Die tödliche Utopie*, (Munich, 2010), p. 268.

had signed up. Each paid a 50 pfennig monthly subscription, which entitled them to apply for tickets to sporting and cultural events sponsored or subsidised by the KdF, such as theatre showings, concerts, chess tournaments, weekend rambles or swimming lessons. Moreover, no actor or singer was permitted to perform in Nazi Germany unless they agreed to give a month of their time, every year, to perform free of charge for KdF audiences.[16] It was clearly no sideshow. In 1937, the year that the *Wilhelm Gustloff* was launched, the KdF staged over 600,000 cultural and sporting events across Germany, which were attended by nearly 50 million participants. By 1939, the

---

[16] William Teeling, "Workless in Germany", in *The Times*, 22 February 1934, p. 15.

last year in which the organisation was fully operative, those figures had almost doubled.[17]

Aside from weekend and evening activities, the KdF also expanded into providing holidays for German workers. It had been one of its key commitments, to provide an annual holiday for every German worker, and it was seriously meant. Holiday provision quickly accounted for a fifth of the organisation's total expenditure. In one of the first of such excursions, a thousand Berlin workers were sent on a chartered train to Bavaria in February 1934. As *The Times* reported, with uncustomary enthusiasm: "they marched from their factories and other places of work, headed by flags and bands in brown uniforms, playing

---

[17] Figures quoted in Dahm et. al., op. cit., p. 268.

lively music. They marched smartly in fours, with suitcases swinging in their hands."[18]

In the five years up to 1939, the KdF organised around 7 million holidays, encompassing one in ten of the German workforce.[19] Such holidays – predominantly within Germany itself – were for the first time made affordable for ordinary working class Germans, many of whom had never been 'on holiday' before. They could be paid for piecemeal by purchasing stamps in a savings book and were heavily subsidised: 9 days in the Erzgebirge, for instance, would cost 25 RM, while 11 days in Frankenwald would set a worker back 22 RM- less than the average

---

[18] "Holiday for 1000 Berlin workers", in *The Times*, 19 February 1934, p. 11.
[19] Rostock & Zadnicek, op. cit., p. 21.

weekly wage.[20] It was in this spirit that the vast resort complex at Prora on the Baltic island of Rügen was conceived; as a place where all Germans would mix and mingle and enjoy the bracing sea air. Rhinelanders would rub shoulders with East Prussians, Frisians with Bavarians, Saxons with Swabians, and all for the bargain price of 18 RM per week. Though it would never receive any Nazi holidaymakers, Prora's huge 4.5km building was constructed to house 20,000 at a time, and serve as a showpiece of the 'New Germany'. Remarkably, it was planned to be only one of four such resorts.[21]

The same logic applied to the construction of the KdF fleet, including the *Wilhelm Gustloff*. It was intended to provide ordinary German

---

[20] Quoted in Irmgard von zur Mühlen, *Urlaub im Dritten Reich: Kraft durch Freude*, TV documentary, 2001.
[21] "The Nazi at Play", in *The Times*, 12 June 1937, p. 13.

workers with the possibility of enjoying a sea-cruise, something which had previously only been available to the very wealthy. In 1937, the year that the *Gustloff* was being fitted-out and was yet to enter service, the KdF fleet of nine vessels made 146 cruises, carrying over 130,000 passengers to destinations from the Baltic Sea to Madeira.[22] Costs, subsidised of course, were affordable; with 59 RM charged for a 5-day tour of the Norwegian fjords and 63 RM for a week in the Mediterranean, rising to 150 RM for a 12-day tour around Italy, and 155 RM for a two-week voyage to Lisbon and Madeira.[23] With average weekly wages at around 30 RM per week, it is easy to see the enormous popular appeal that such trips had. The Nazi newspaper, the *Völkischer*

---

[22] Schön, *Traumschiffe*, op. cit., p. 34.
[23] Ibid., p. 52.

Beobachter, summed up the attraction, and the political message, in one simple picture story in March 1938. Beneath an image of workers relaxing in the sunshine on the deck of the Gustloff, the caption read: "Marxism only talks about it, but National Socialism delivers the worker's dearest wish: a carefree annual holiday in which to laze to your heart's content."[24]

It was no surprise perhaps, that the *Wilhelm Gustloff*'s first voyage, in late March 1938, was a propaganda exercise. Departing from Hamburg on a 48-hour 'trial cruise' to Heligoland and back via the Danish coast, the vessel carried a thousand Austrians as well as 300 teenage girls of the *Bund Deutscher Mädel* – or 'League of German Girls' – and some 165 journalists. Given that Austria had only been

---

[24] *Völkischer Beobachter*, 29 March 1938, p. 3.

annexed by Germany two weeks before, it was evidently considered beneficial to demonstrate the tangible benefits of belonging to the Nazi Reich to a select group of Austrian workers. For many of them the cruise certainly made for an unforgettable experience; dancing the night away, relaxing on deck or gazing out across a sea that some of them had never seen before. As one passenger confessed to a waiting journalist: "I can't quite grasp what has happened to me." It was said that he had tears in his eyes.[25] Others shared the sentiment. Upon their return to Hamburg, the Austrian passengers collectively penned Hitler a telegram to thank him for the "overwhelming camaraderie" that they had experienced aboard

---

[25] Schön, Traumschiffe, op. cit., p. 35.

this "National Socialist tour de force, the proudest ship in the world".[26]

Propaganda was never far from the *Wilhelm Gustloff*, even when it was unintended. On 2 April 1938, it left Hamburg en route to the English Channel where it was scheduled to meet three other KdF cruise ships and accompany them back to port. However, after a severe deterioration in the weather on day two of the voyage, the *Gustloff* found itself involved in a maritime emergency when it intercepted an SOS call from a British freighter, the *Pegaway*, which was taking on water close to the Dutch island of Terschelling and was in danger of sinking. Hurrying to the rescue, the *Gustloff* succeeded in bringing the 19 crew of the *Pegaway* to safety in her motor launch just before the freighter sank.

[26] Quoted in ibid., p. 36.

Predictably, the press had a field day. Many German newspapers put the story on their front pages and pointedly praised the *Gustloff*'s crew for "saving the English from peril on the seas".[27] The British press concurred: "German Heroes" proclaimed the *Western Morning News*, while the London *Evening Standard* got itself in a muddle, describing the *Gustloff* as a "Nazi Joy Ship". The Pathé newsreel report opined – somewhat optimistically – that the *Pegaway* episode had shown that "the brotherhood of the sea knows no political frontiers."[28]

Soon after, with the plaudits still ringing in the crew's ears, the *Gustloff* was called to attend another propaganda opportunity, this time an official one. Following Hitler's hasty

[27] *Völkischer Beobachter*, 5 April 1938, p. 1.
[28] *Evening Standard*, 4 April 1938, and April 1938 footage from Pathé at https://www.youtube.com/watch?v=NhO1Z_DhraI

annexation of Austria in March 1938, a plebiscite was organised for the following month in an attempt to head off international criticism and give the *Anschluss* a veneer of legitimacy. The vote was also extended to those Germans living abroad, and consequently over a hundred vessels were dispatched to enable Germans (and Austrians) around the world to cast their votes. In a propaganda masterstroke, the *Wilhelm Gustloff*, the pride of the German fleet and the recent hero of the *Pegaway* rescue, was sent to London, where she would moor at Tilbury in the Thames estuary and take UK-resident Germans and Austrians on board, before sailing out beyond British territorial waters where the plebiscite could take place.

The plan, thought brilliantly simple, was nonetheless fraught with complications. For one thing, the vast majority of Austrians and Germans in the UK were refugees from Nazi persecution. Austrian and German Jews were explicitly barred from taking part in the plebiscite, but even amongst their gentile fellows, the oppositional mood was such that very few of them had any interest in registering their presence with the German Embassy in London and then stepping aboard a Nazi ship to be sailed out into international waters. They feared – with some justification – that they might be taken back to Hitler's Germany, or at the very least that they might encounter difficulties getting back into the UK. There were also a few protests against the presence of the *Gustloff* in the London approaches, with a Trade Union picket set up at London's St Pancras station denouncing the presence of the vessel as "confounded insolence and propaganda". It was no surprise then, that only 2,000 of the estimated 35,000 Germans and Austrians then resident in the United Kingdom turned up to vote.[29]

Those that did were treated to a fine day out at Germany's expense. Once the vessel left British waters, those Nazi officials present changed into their uniforms, placards were unveiled, and speeches were held. As elsewhere in Greater Germany, even the voting slip was biased in favour of Hitler; with a large circle in the centre of the sheet for a 'Yes' vote, and a smaller, off-set space for those that dared to vote 'No'.[30] Away from the politics, the day had a party atmosphere, with oompah bands, cabaret performers and demonstrations of

---

[29] Bill Niven, "Die *Gustloff* in London", in Bill Niven (ed.), *Die Wilhelm Gustloff*, (Halle, 2011), pp. 65-67.
[30] See the image at
http://en.wikipedia.org/wiki/Anschluss#mediaviewer/File:Stim
mzettel-Anschluss.jpg

gymnastics by the Hitler Youth and German Girls' League. There was subsidised beer and as much food as the conscientious voter could eat. Indeed a cartoon in the left-wing *Daily Herald* summed up the seduction perfectly, with a plump German saying "Ja" to more food, more drink, a cigar, another beer and finally, to Hitler's annexation of Austria.[31] The only surprise of the day was that ten of the 2,000 voters present voted against.

Ten days after that Thames outing, on April 21st 1938, the *Wilhelm Gustloff* finally made her maiden voyage, departing with 1,465 excited passengers for a two-week cruise via Lisbon to Madeira. Yet, even then, controversy and ill-fortune were following in her wake. One day in to the cruise, the vessel's captain,

---

[31] *Daily Herald*, 12 April 1938, reproduced in Niven (ed.), op. cit., p. 69.

58 year-old Carl Lübbe, suffered a fatal heart attack on the bridge, plunging the ship into a 48-hour period of mourning, with music and dancing cancelled and a blank 'events' page in the ship's programme. While Lübbe was taken ashore at Dover, to be replaced in Lisbon by a temporary captain; Friedrich Petersen, the *Gustloff* continued her voyage westward, flanked by the KdF ships *Sierra Cordoba* and *Der Deutsche*.

Once underway, the passengers would doubtless have been seduced by the *Wilhelm Gustloff*'s opulent facilities and décor. For the many aboard who had perhaps never even stayed in a hotel before, the vessel – with its 10 decks – must have made a hugely impressive sight. True to its 'classless' design, all of its 616 cabins across four decks were built to two patterns – whether 2 or 4-bed – and all had a sea view, with toilet facilities being shared. In addition, it boasted seven bars, two restaurants, dance and concert halls, a library, a smoking room, a hair-dressing salon and a swimming pool – all of which were accessible to the passengers, in line with the vessel's 'national-socialist' ethos.[32]

As one might expect, life on board was strictly ordered. The day started with reveille at 6.20am, and for early risers a session of exercises was scheduled on the sundeck ten minutes later. Breakfast was served from 7-8am; and for half an hour after it ended, a selection of popular music would be broadcast via the ship's public address system. Shortly after 9am a briefing would be given by the KdF tour guide, explaining what could be expected

---

[32] Heinz Schön, *Die Gustloff Katastrophe*, (Stuttgart, 2002), pp. 67-69.

from the next port of call. Passengers were not always permitted to leave the ship when in harbour, and it seems to have depended largely on the destination. Less-developed or more 'German-friendly' locations such as Portugal, Spain, Italy or Libya preferred for shore excursions over those such as Norway; which might feasibly have dented any nascent sense of German superiority.[33] Like Lisbon, Madeira was evidently considered a 'safe' destination, as passengers were issued with a rudimentary map of the island, as well as an excursion pass and a ticket for a guided tour of the capital, Funchal.[34]

After the morning briefing, passengers would be treated to organised entertainment on deck,

---

[33] Sascha Howind, "Das 'Traumschiff' für die 'Volksgemeinschaft'? Die *Gustloff* und die soziale Propaganda des Dritten Reiches", in Niven (ed.), op. cit., p. 33.
[34] See the items displayed at the http://www.wilhelmgustloffmuseum.com/maiden_voyage.html

perhaps some folk dancing or a musical performance. Lectures were also common, with the ship itself being a common theme. On the vessel's maiden voyage, diarist Elisabeth Dietrich attended a lecture on "The machinery of the MS *Wilhelm Gustloff*", and dutifully recorded that the ship had 4 eight-cylinder diesel engines, noting their bore, stroke, optimum rpm. and power output. The twin propellers, she added, had a 5 metre diameter, weighed 15 tonnes each, and were attached to a 75 metre drive shaft. She wrote, with regret, that she was unable to listen to "this interesting presentation" to the end, as she was called to lunch.[35] One has to admire her technological prowess.

Being called to lunch was not an excuse to get away. Mealtimes were strictly delineated

---

[35] See extracts from Elisabeth Dietrich's diary at ibid.

aboard the *Gustloff*. Lunch was served in two sittings, between 11.30am and 12.30pm; followed by another presentation in the concert hall. It has been estimated that, for each mealtime, the ship's kitchens prepared 400 litres of soup, 5,000 sausages, 400 kilos of vegetables and a metric tonne of potatoes. In addition, 10,000 slices of bread were cut each day, 5,000 bread rolls were baked, as well as 4,000 Danish pastries. Over 3,000 tonnes of drinking water was stored in the ship's funnel. And, after meals, 35,000 plates, as well as countless items of cutlery and glassware all had to be washed.[36]

In the afternoon, passengers were free to relax on deck, in their cabins or in one of the communal rooms. A flavour of life aboard was

---

[36] Schön, *Katastrophe*, op. cit., p. 68.

given by a journalist, who shared that maiden voyage:

"It is Sunday. Every day on this ship is a Sunday. The Spanish coast is sixty miles away, and the Bay of Biscay is being kind to us; the dark blue sea, here and there topped with a white foam, is peaceful and calm. And the broad sundeck of the *Wilhelm Gustloff* has become a meeting point for all of Germany; all the dialects of the Reich, from Königsberg to Vienna, are represented."[37]

After such exertions, passengers were treated to the customary 'coffee and cake' at 4pm before the evening's entertainment began an hour later with a concert by the ship's orchestra. Supper was served from 7pm – again in two sittings – before music and dancing took over all the communal areas of the ship from

---

[37] Heinrich Zerkaulen, quoted in ibid., p. 92.

8.30pm. By midnight all revelry would come to an end with a strict 'lights out'.[38]

Life on board the *Gustloff* was not all fun and games, however. Political content was never absent entirely, and was either delivered within the presentations of the KdF resident tour guide, or – more explicitly – via the vessel's network of 138 loud-speakers, which, as well as broadcasting music and announcements, was used to relay recordings of Hitler's speeches.[39] Of course, the vast majority of passengers, almost by definition, would have been positively predisposed towards Nazism and so receptive to the message; and for those that were in any doubt, the regime made sure to

---

[38] Schön, *Katastrophe*, op. cit., pp. 103-4.
[39] Ibid., p. 67.

have its spies aboard, listening out for dissenting opinions.[40]

Each one of the *Wilhelm Gustloff*'s voyages carried with it representatives of the Gestapo or SS security service (SD) to monitor public opinion. As one such agent noted in his report, his tasks were "to observe the passengers primarily with regard to their attitude towards the current government", to watch their "political demeanour" and to liaise where necessary with the *Gustloff*'s KdF staff.[41] In most cases, there was not much of a 'political' nature to report; the majority of SS summaries noted that the atmosphere on the vessel was exemplary, and the voyage a great success. However a number of lesser matters evidently troubled the Gestapo agents, not least amongst

---

[40] Howind, op. cit., p. 34.
[41] SS internal report dated 8 August 1938, Bundesarchiv, Berlin, R58/948/47. With thanks to Bill Niven.

them the evident disinclination of many passengers to use the 'Hitler greeting' – the outstretched arm along with the "Heil Hitler" – with many preferring to avoid any formal greeting at all. Other agents noted with concern that many of the senior personnel on the *Gustloff* were Freemasons.[42]

A more serious problem identified aboard the *Gustloff* was that of class. All passengers were required to be members of the KdF, of course, and according to National Socialist propaganda, they were supposed to be ordinary workers; representatives of the German proletariat to be weaned away from their mistaken faith in the precepts of Marx and Lenin. However, KdF organisers increasingly saw their activities being infiltrated by the

---

[42] Ibid., R58/948/46 and R58/948/48, 15 August, 1938 & R58/948/121, 28 August 1939.

middle class. In Kassel in 1934, for instance, the local KdF banned the participation of the middle classes in its holiday excursions, because, it said, such "parasites and spongers" were perfectly able to pay for a holiday themselves.[43]

Given the costs involved, and the high profile of the cruises, the problem was even more acute aboard the *Gustloff*, and moreover, given the close proximity of all passengers for an extended period, class differences were made all the more obvious. In fact, despite the propaganda, the majority of the 75,000 passengers who travelled aboard the *Gustloff* were white collar workers and those that modern parlance might call "the sharp-elbowed middle class". SS statistics from the *Gustloff*'s

---

[43] Quoted in "German Workers' Trips" in *The Times*, 19 September 1934, p. 9.

final voyage in August 1939, showed that only 11% of passengers earned below average income.[44] The KdF's own statistics, moreover, concluded that in the five years that sea cruises were offered across the organisation, only 17% of the total of 750,000 passengers described themselves as 'workers', with a further 10% identifying themselves as 'artisans' and only 1.5% being agricultural labourers. The remainder were solidly middle and upper-middle class; academics, middle and senior management and civil servants.[45]

This, naturally perhaps, could be the cause of some tension. Far from all of the KdF's passengers discovering their shared sense of Germanness, it seems class continued to define many of them. One voyage to the Norwegian

[44] Bundesarchiv, op. cit., R58/948/122, 28 August 1939.
[45] Schön, *Traumschiffe*, op. cit., p. 53.

fjords, in August 1938, saw such perennial differences surfacing "in particularly crass form". As the SS agent noted in his report, the trip included – alongside the ordinary 'workers' – a number of passengers whose costs were paid, either as clients of particular firms or as the 'honoured guests' of the Nazi Gauleiter for Saarpfalz, Josef Bürckel. Such guests, the SS agent continued, not only declined to mix with the other passengers, they also demanded special treatment; for instance requesting a private room in the bar. In addition, some of the ladies present were noticed to have made as many as *six* costume changes in a single day, which – it was noted – rather irritated the 'ordinary' holidaymakers in their midst. The conclusion, for the SS agent at least, was clear: "such guests should not be on KdF ships".[46]

Aside from such concerns, the *Gustloff* proved wildly popular. And, to spread the word still further, a propaganda film crew accompanied her maiden voyage, producing a 20-minute film optimistically entitled *Schiff ohne Klassen* – "The Classless Ship" – which was shown in German cinemas in 1938. Beautifully shot, with original sound throughout, it gives a highly polished and propagandistic view of life aboard the *Gustloff* – all comradely Germans, technological excellence and tinned peaches – topped off with a sun-soaked bus tour of Lisbon. It cannot

---

[46] Quoted in Bundesarchiv, op. cit., R58/948/47-49, 8 August 1938.

have failed to attract a new crop of eager passengers.[47]

After the success of her maiden voyage – bar the death of her captain, of course – the *Wilhelm Gustloff* settled into what was planned to be her annual routine. After a spring of visits to Madeira, she would tour the Norwegian fjords over the summer, before heading for the Mediterranean in the autumn, where she would spend the winter touring Italy, with her passengers arriving by train to her adopted home port of Genoa. This routine was broken only by occasional 'business voyages' where the vessel was taken over by a single concern or organisation,[48] or by the propaganda demands of the Nazi regime in Berlin, which

---

[47] "Schiff ohne Klassen" available at
www.youtube.com/watch?v=sPLK3yPjNes
[48] See the Wilhelm Gustloff Museum at
http://www.wilhelmgustloffmuseum.com/speisekarten_-_menus_2.html

liked to use the *Gustloff* as a high profile floating hotel for its citizens, for instance during the 'Lingiad' gymnastics festival, held in Stockholm in July 1939.[49]

Perhaps the most famous use of the *Gustloff* in this propaganda capacity occurred earlier that summer, in May 1939, when the vessel – along with the other ships of the KdF fleet – received a mysterious order to sail west out of Hamburg, with no passengers and a skeleton crew. In due course, a second order was given: to sail to the Spanish port of Vigo, where the fleet was to collect and repatriate the Condor Legion.

The Condor Legion was the name given to the approximately 25,000 German airmen and soldiers who had 'volunteered' for service in

---

[49] "Gymnasts festival in Stockholm", in *The Times*, 22 July 1939, p. 11

support of General Franco in the Spanish Civil War. The first of their number arrived in the summer of 1936 and assisted with the crucial task of airlifting Franco's "Army of Africa" across the Straits of Gibraltar to the Spanish mainland. Thereafter, German manpower and materiel in Spain multiplied, such that in time, six squadrons of aircraft as well as ground crew, signals and intelligence units were present. In addition, two German armoured units with over 100 tanks were also active in the Nationalist cause. German help was to prove vital to Franco's success, assisting at the battles of Madrid, Jarama and Belchite, and carrying out the infamous bombing of the Basque town of Guernica in 1937.

By the spring of 1939, Franco was victorious. The Legion had completed its operations and its remaining 10,000 or so personnel were to be brought back to Germany. Amid great ceremonial, the soldiers and airmen boarded the KdF fleet in Vigo harbour on the 25th May; the *Wilhelm Gustloff* alone taking some 1,400 passengers. After the rigours of warfare, the *Gustloff* offered a slightly more genteel environment, with the usual lectures on offer, as well as films, musical evenings and boxing on deck. Doubtless refreshed, the soldiers returned to a heroes' welcome, being met by a flotilla of warships off the Frisian coast, and escorted into the Elbe estuary. At Neumühlen, to the west of Hamburg, Göring himself took the salute of the returning troops from the quayside, and coastal artillery batteries blasted out their welcome.[50]

---

[50] "German Volunteers home from Spain" in *Hull Daily Mail*, 31 May 1939, p. 1.

After the excitement of bringing the Condor Legion home, the summer of 1939 passed uneventfully with the *Wilhelm Gustloff* returning to its regular programme of touring the Norwegian fjords. With the clouds of war gathering, however, that routine was soon to be interrupted once more. On 24th August, while the *Gustloff* was moored in the Sognefjord, north of Bergen, a coded message informed her captain that the voyage was to be cut short and the ship was being recalled to Hamburg. As the news was passed on to the passengers, earnest discussions broke out all over the ship, not least about the possible significance of the Nazi-Soviet Pact, which had been signed the day before. A vivid demonstration of the new reality was given when the *Gustloff* was briefly intercepted by a Royal Navy destroyer. Two days later, on the 26th August, she docked safely in Hamburg; her future – like that of the wider continent – shrouded in doubt.

*

The 417 crew of the *Wilhelm Gustloff* were not kept in the dark for long. The vast majority of them were released from their posts already on the second day of the war, leaving only a skeleton maintenance, engineering and navigation crew to man the ship. The *Gustloff* herself had been requisitioned into the German Navy the day before and was subordinated to the Navy command in Hamburg on the 5th September as a Navy Auxiliary Vessel. Four days after that, her fate was decided; she was to be refitted as a hospital ship.

In truth, the decision to refit the *Wilhelm Gustloff* was one that had been made some time earlier. Hitler had planned his expansionist foreign policy course right from the outset of his rule in Germany. At a meeting with his General Staff only days after coming to power in 1933, he had outlined his plan to militarily expand eastwards, creating *Lebensraum* for the growing German population at the expense of those he perceived to be lesser nations.[51] Though the precise course and circumstances of the war were as yet unknown, it was naturally assumed by all those senior personnel in Hitler's *Reich* that the conflict would bring with it a similar level of military casualties as the First World War had done. Consequently, already in November 1936, the German General Staff had reckoned with needing seven hospital ships in the event of conflict, able to cope with around 3,000 injured soldiers per

---

[51] See Gerhard Weinberg, *Hitler's Foreign Policy 1933-1939: The Road to World War Two*, (Chicago, 1981), pp. 23-24.

week.[52] Given her size, as soon as the *Wilhelm Gustloff* was launched the following year, she would have been included in such planning.

So, with the outbreak of war, the *Gustloff* was duly refitted; her interior remodelled to accommodate 500 hospital beds as well as various medical facilities such as operating theatres and treatment rooms. Her exterior, meanwhile, was painted white, with a 90cm dark green stripe along her flanks, from stem to stern, and a red cross adorning her funnel, all in accordance with the Geneva Convention.

In this guise – as "Hospital Ship D" – the *Wilhelm Gustloff* arrived at Danzig in the last days of September, just as the German campaign against Poland was drawing to a victorious conclusion. Nonetheless, she served her purpose; and, in a curious twist, was first of

---

[52] Schön, *Katastrophe*, op. cit., p. 119.

all given the task of evacuating 685 wounded Polish soldiers westwards to Rendsburg, near Kiel. Some, it seems, were unimpressed with the *Gustloff* being used in this way and a musical welcoming committee at Rendsburg was cancelled, when it was discovered that Polish wounded were aboard the vessel rather than German.[53] Returning to Danzig in early October to await instructions, the *Gustloff* berthed opposite the battle-scarred remains of the Polish fort on the Westerplatte, where the opening shots of the war had been fired little over a month earlier.

In due course, a use of sorts was found for the *Gustloff*; she was to be moored at Gdynia – which the Nazis renamed Gotenhafen (or "Goths' Harbour") – where she would serve as an emergency floating hospital, held in reserve

---

[53] Ibid., p. 129.

in case of an Allied attack on Danzig. She soon found another purpose. After the Nazi-Soviet Pact of the previous summer had divided Eastern Europe between Hitler and Stalin, thousands of ethnic Germans (*Volksdeutsche*) who had formerly lived in those regions ceded to the Soviets were brought "home" to the Reich, in a mass evacuation beginning in the autumn of 1939. As one might expect, the German authorities treated the evacuation as a propaganda exercise, and the sending of the cruise liners *Sierra Cordoba* and *General von Steuben* to the region was an essential part of the show. Despite the seriousness of their predicament, many Baltic Germans were overwhelmed by the glamour and opulence of the vessels, and were excited by the prospect of a sea voyage. One wrote home explaining that the décor of the ship was "so luxurious, we thought we were in heaven". Another said "Is this Adolf Hitler's ship? Has he many ships? His ship is very beautiful."[54]

The *Gustloff* was not included in the evacuation, but was part of the reception. Due to its proximity to the Baltic States, where many of the *Volksdeutsche* lived, Gotenhafen served as one of the main ports of entry, so facilities were set up there for the administrative processing and medical screening of the evacuees.[55] Those among them who required medical treatment, therefore, could find themselves aboard the *Wilhelm Gustloff*, in what was doubtless an impressive entrée to their new lives as citizens of Hitler's Reich.

---

[54] Quoted in Bill Niven (ed.), op. cit., p. 79.
[55] Maria Fiebrandt, *Auslese für die Siedlergesellschaft: Die Einbeziehung Volksdeutscher in Die NS-Erbgesundheitspolitik im Kontext der Umsiedlungen 1939-1945*, (Göttingen, 2014), p. 289.

For the Poles living beyond the dockside in Gotenhafen, meanwhile, life was rather more brutal. Condemned to an existence as second-class citizens, they were already being deported to the 'Polish reserve' of the General Government, while those among them who were considered a threat to German rule were earmarked for imprisonment in the infamous concentration camp at Stutthof, east of Danzig, or simply executed. Under the Nazis, Gotenhafen was scheduled to become a purely German city, but the process was characterised by chaos, violence and chronic mismanagement, with populations being sorted and sifted while infrastructure was packaged up and sent westwards. A visiting Swedish journalist quipped in 1939 that the dislocation and disruption in Gotenhafen was such that it should have been renamed "Totenhafen" (the 'Harbour of the Dead').[56]

Six months later, while the ethnic reordering of central Europe continued apace, the *Wilhelm Gustloff* was once again pressed into service as a hospital ship for the military. When German forces invaded Denmark and Norway in April 1940, she made two trips to Oslo to evacuate German wounded. Then, as Hitler planned "Operation Sealion"; his seaborne invasion of Britain, later that summer, the vessel was moved to Bremerhaven in readiness, only for the operation to be cancelled due to the stubborn desire of the British to defend themselves. After returning to Oslo for a third time, that autumn, the *Gustloff* sailed back to Gotenhafen in November 1940, where most of

---

[56] Halik Kochanski, *The Eagle Unbowed: Poland and the Poles in the Second World War*, (London, 2013), p. 106.

her remaining crew were dismissed and her medical equipment removed. As a hospital ship, she had treated over 3,000 injured soldiers, carried out 12,000 clinical examinations, 1,700 x-rays and 347 operations, but now that role too was at an end.[57]

Despite being only three years old, the *Wilhelm Gustloff* found herself in limbo. With the war well under way, there would clearly be no KdF pleasure cruises in the immediate future, yet the campaigns for which she had undergone an expensive refit were already seemingly at an end. Now, repainted in camouflage grey, she appeared doomed to obscurity; moored permanently at Gotenhafen and destined for use as a floating barracks. Increasingly, she must have looked to her masters in Berlin to be something of a white

[57] Schön, *Katastrophe*, op. cit., p. 134.

elephant. Alongside her sister ship, the *Robert Ley*, and the vast, unused KdF holiday complex at Prora on the Baltic coast, she was a costly reminder of a bygone age; before the fledgling *Volksgemeinschaft* was sent to war.

Yet, though it is tempting to see the *Gustloff* moored in Gotenhafen as a vessel languishing in provincial insignificance; washed up by the tides of war, she was nonetheless soon to be part of a strategically vital undertaking. Germany had entered World War Two with the largest U-boat fleet of any combatant nation and it was seen as a crucial weapon in combating the economic advantage of the Americans and British. Only by disrupting trans-Atlantic supply routes, it was thought, could Germany ultimately expect to defeat her Western enemies. But, given that U-boats were being sunk by Allied forces at a rate of 2 per month in 1940,[58] new vessels had to be built and new crews had to be trained, far away from the dangers of combat.

The eastern Baltic Sea, safely beyond the range of most Allied aircraft, provided the perfect arena both for the construction of submarines and the schooling of submariners. Danzig, for instance, was home to two shipyards – the Danziger Werft and the Schichau – which were central to U-boat production, contributing over 150 of the 700 completed Type VII vessels that were the mainstay of the German wartime U-boat fleet. Nearby Gotenhafen, meanwhile, became home to two U-boat training flotillas – the 22nd and 27th – and was the base port of the two *Unterseeboots-Lehrdivision* (U-boat training division). The *Wilhelm Gustloff* served as the

---

division's floating barracks, home to around 1,000 cadets and staff.[59]

Life for the cadets stationed on the *Gustloff* was comfortable rather than luxurious. Stripped of her medical equipment and converted now to a purely dormitory function, the ship was basically furnished – but still retained many of its more sumptuous fittings and features, such as a theatre hall, which could be used for film showings and lectures for the crews. Paradoxically, the conflict for which the cadets were training must have seemed a long way off. As one of those present later recalled: "apart from the radio, we heard and saw nothing of war."[60]

Cadets would generally spend a full six months training, during which time they would

---

[59] Gordon Williamson, *U-Boat Bases and Bunkers; 1940-45*, (Oxford, 2003), p. 30. Schön, *Katastrophe*, op. cit., p. 137.
[60] Schön, *Katastrophe*, op. cit., p. 137.

be taught all aspects of the submariner's art, as well as receiving a refresher course on naval basics, such as signalling, Morse and navigation. Training for officer cadets was much more rigorous, consisting of two lengthy secondments – to a sailing ship and then a cruiser – followed by further additional courses of instruction, some of which were held aboard the *Cap Arcona*, which was also moored in Gotenhafen. The submariner's training was initially theoretical and taught in the classroom, before the cadets graduated to working on a mock-up of a submarine's control room, and finally to a working U-boat, usually an older model set aside for the purpose. Then the crews would take to the open sea of the Baltic to put their training into action, as Werner Viehs recalled:

"One August morning in 1944, on the Bay of Danzig, we went out for the first time on a submarine. The time before we had spent learning all the necessary procedures. We had practiced on the mock-up until we could do everything in our sleep, without thinking ... Leaving the harbour, we heard "Alarm! Dive! Action stations!" The hatch was shut, the diesel engines switched off and disengaged, the vents closed, the fuel supply cut off... Over the loudspeaker came readiness reports from all sections of the ship."[61]

In this way, cadets had the opportunity to train on some of the most iconic U-boats in the German fleet. One of the vessels seconded to the 22nd Training Flotilla at Gotenhafen, for instance, was U-96; a Type VIIC, which had

---

[61] See eye-witness account at
https://www.dhm.de/lemo/zeitzeugen/werner-viehs-u-boot-ausbildung-in-gotenhafen-und-pillau-1944.html

sunk 27 ships totalling over 180,000 tons in her two year career on active service. Not only was U-96 one of the most successful German U-boats of the war, she would later become immortalised as the vessel featured in the film "*Das Boot*". The origin of the film was that U-96 was accompanied on one of her eleven patrols by a young war correspondent named Lothar-Günther Buchheim, who would later use his experiences to write the novel "*Das Boot*", upon which the film was based.

In addition, the cadets had the benefit of being trained by some of the highest-scoring 'aces' of the U-boat service. One of them was Heinrich "Ajax" Bleichrodt, who came to Gotenhafen in the summer of 1943, after a three-year career in which he had sunk 150,000 tons of shipping and become one of only twelve U-boat commanders to be awarded the prestigious 'U-boat War Badge with Diamonds'. At Gotenhafen, Bleichrodt taught tactics to the officer cadets for a year, before being promoted to the overall command of 22nd Training Flotilla.

Another luminary was Erich Topp, who as captain of the Type VII U-552 – known as the "Red Devil Boat" – achieved huge success sinking a total of 192,000 tons and 35 vessels. Controversially, one of his 'kills' was the American destroyer USS *Reuben James*, which was sunk off Iceland in October 1941, six weeks *before* America entered the war.[62] Transferred to a shore command in the autumn of 1942 as commander of 27th Training Flotilla based at Gotenhafen, Topp was responsible for overseeing the tactical training of cadet crews.

---

[62] Gordon Williamson, *Kriegsmarine U-boats 1939-1945*, (Oxford, 2002), p. 24.

A highlight for Topp was doubtless the visit of Hitler to the port, in May 1941, during which he boarded one of Topp's old boats – U-57 – which was being used as a training vessel.[63]

For all their high profile visitors and illustrious instructors, the cadets at Gotenhafen were embarking on an increasingly perilous existence. Those – the majority – that were sent out to join Type VII U-boats, joined a typical crew of 44 ratings plus eight officers, which would carry out each 'patrol' of up to three months, scouring the Atlantic on the hunt for Allied convoys. Strictly speaking, the Type VII was a submersible rather than a true submarine; it spent most of its time on the surface, powered by its twin diesel engines, and only submerged either to attack or to avoid attack.

[63] Laurence Paterson, *First U-boat Flotilla*, (Barnsley, 2001), p. 65.

Nonetheless, it was scarcely comfortable. Squeezed into the cramped interior of the boat, working in 8-hour shifts and sleeping in hammocks slung alongside their torpedoes, the crews would rarely see daylight and veterans joked that they would soon smell their comrades before they saw them. Yet, despite such difficulties, in the opening phase of the war – known to German crews as the "Happy Time" – U-boats cut such a swathe through Allied shipping that Britain's survival was seriously endangered. Churchill himself would later confess that the only thing that truly frightened him during World War Two was the peril of the German U-boats.[64]

Yet, after May 1943, when superior Allied intelligence and counter-measures forced a

[64] Quoted in Nigel West, *Historical Dictionary of Naval Intelligence*, (London, 2010), p. 322.

turning point in the Battle of the Atlantic, joining a U-boat crew became akin to signing your own death warrant. From that point, U-boat losses multiplied; more U-boats were lost in 1943, than had been lost in the whole war hitherto and the average monthly loss of 3 U-boats between 1939 and 1942 rocketed to 20 for the period thereafter.[65]

The experience of the cadet crews from Gotenhafen can perhaps best be illustrated by the fate of a single boat. U-109 was launched in Bremen in the autumn of 1940. The following summer, she and her crew underwent tactical training at Gotenhafen, including two simulated convoy battles out in the Baltic, before being assigned to 2nd Flotilla, based at Lorient on the French Atlantic coast. A Type IXB boat, she was larger than the more

---

[65] See statistics at http://www.uboat.net/fates/losses/chart.htm

common Type VII, so was theoretically better suited to operations in the open Atlantic, where she undertook 9 patrols – mostly under the command of Heinrich Bleichrodt – averaging 42 days each, and sinking a total of 86,000 tons of Allied shipping. The end of U-109 came in the spring of 1943, when under her new commander; the 27-year-old Joachim Schramm, she was spotted off the south-west of Ireland by a British Liberator aircraft. While trying to carry out a crash dive, she was damaged by depth charges dropped by the Liberator, and briefly rose to the surface before sinking again out of sight. All 52 officers and crew were lost.[66]

The fate of U-109 was by no means uncommon. Of the 859 U-boats that left

---

[66] See Axel Niestlé, *German U-Boat Losses During World Wat Two*, (Barnsley, 2014), p. 118 and http://www.uboat.net/boats/u109.htm

German bases for front-line service, 757 were lost. Of these, 429 – exactly half of the total that saw action – went down with their entire crews.[67] It should come as no surprise, then, that of the 39,000 officers and men involved in the German U-boat offensive, 32,000 – fully 82% – were listed as killed or missing at war's end.[68] Many of those men would have been trained in Gotenhafen and would have spent time aboard the *Gustloff*.

In the safety of Gotenhafen, however, the war rarely intruded. Beyond the range of Allied bombers for most of the war, the town – and its port – were only rarely targeted. However, one raid – on 9 October 1943 – hit particularly hard when over 100 B-17s and B-24s of the US 8th Army Air Force bombed the harbour area in

[67] Niestlé, op. cit., pp. 3-4.
[68] John Ellis, *The World War Two Databook*, (London, 2003), p. 254.

the early afternoon. Despite stubborn flak defence, the Americans succeeded in causing considerable damage on the ground, and in the water; the hospital ship *Stuttgart* was sunk, along with a minesweeper, an anti-submarine vessel, a U-boat supply ship and a number of freighters and tugs. The *Wilhelm Gustloff* was also damaged, sustaining a 1.5-metre gash in her hull from a near miss.[69]

Beyond that, and the small matter of its U-boat crews disappearing to an uncertain fate, Gotenhafen and its barrack ships were largely untouched by the war. In the final weeks of 1944, however, that changed. As submariner Paul Vollrath recalled, it was in December "that training was completely stopped and instead trainees, staff and old submarine crews were armed with spades and shovels and off we

---

[69] Schön, *Katastrophe*, op. cit., pp. 138-9.

went into the outer suburbs of [Gotenhafen] to dig tank trenches."[70] Though Vollrath's faith in the "final victory" was miraculously undented by that experience, it was nonetheless clear to all those with eyes in their head that Germany's war was fast approaching its savage endgame.

The Red Army had already crossed the East Prussian frontier two months earlier, in October 1944, but their westward advance had been temporarily stayed while the Balkans had been cleared. Nonetheless, events in East Prussia that month, would give a grim foretaste of what was to come for civilians. In the village of Nemmersdorf, on 21st October 1944, conquering Soviet forces engaged in an orgy of violence before being briefly repelled. The resulting carnage of rape and murder, in which

---

[70] Vollrath's testimony at:
http://wilhelmgustloff.com/stories_sinking_PVollrath.htm

as many as 30 German locals and French POWs were slaughtered, was a gift to Nazi propaganda. Joseph Goebbels put the Nemmersdorf massacre in his newsreels that month, in the mistaken belief that knowledge of Soviet brutality would stiffen German resolve and will to resist. In many cases it had the opposite effect, spurring a mass flight of civilians from those territories that stood in the Red Army's way. So it was that, already in December 1944, large numbers of German refugees were congregating in the Baltic ports – such as Gotenhafen – seeking a way west. As Paul Vollrath recalled, they "reported rape, murder and untold atrocities and it was hard to believe that all these reports were far-fetched fantasies and imagined dreams … Their looks and the state in which they arrived obviously spoke of a severe urgency."[71]

Vollrath was not mistaken. Hundreds of thousands of East Prussian civilians were already packing up their belongings, in some cases leaving villages and properties that their families had inhabited for centuries, and heading west by any means possible. Yet, despite the evident urgency of the hour, their predicament was still far down the Nazi regime's list of priorities, and though official evacuation plans had been drawn up, they were held back in favour of hysterical calls for popular resistance. Those gathering in desperation on the quayside at Gotenhafen and

---

[71] Ibid.

elsewhere, were at risk of incurring the wrath of their own side.[72]

That growing human tide was only made more pressing in mid-January 1945, when Soviet forces renewed their westward offensive, breaking out from their bridgeheads over the Vistula river in central Poland, to strike towards the river Oder. Given their huge superiority in men and materiel, and the advantage that the still-frozen ground lent their tank-borne advance, progress was swift and Red Army units quickly found themselves almost within striking distance of Berlin, with their opponents in headlong retreat. In the north, meanwhile, on the Baltic coast, East Prussia was finally cut off when Soviet forces reached the sea at Tolkemit on the 26th

[72] Heinrich Schwendemann, "Schickt Schiffe!" in *Die Zeit*, 13 January, 2005.

January. For those who found themselves just west of that point – in Danzig, or Gotenhafen – evacuation was finally, slowly, becoming a reality.

Eager to evacuate key military personnel, and ensure that no sensitive technology fell into Soviet hands, the order had been given five days earlier, on the 21st January, that the 2nd U-Boat Training Division, based at Gotenhafen, was to be evacuated westwards, using its barracks ships – among them the *Cap Arcona* and the *Wilhelm Gustloff* – for the purpose. Boarding was to begin on January 24th. Across East Prussia; from Hela, Danzig, Königsberg, Memel and Pillau, countless ships were to be requisitioned to remove military wounded and keep remaining troops supplied, that they might continue the fight against the Red Army. The plan was codenamed "Operation

Hannibal" and it would become the largest seaborne evacuation in history.

"Operation Hannibal" rarely gets the serious discussion that it deserves. It was most certainly a remarkable feat of logistics. Within little over four months, in wartime, some 790 vessels of the German merchant and civil fleet – from fishing boats to icebreakers – crossed the Baltic Sea, ferrying what contemporaries estimated at 2 million evacuees and wounded servicemen westwards, out of danger.[73] Some made repeated journeys: the cruise liner *Deutschland*, for instance, made seven crossings, bringing some 70,000 to safety; the 3,000 tonne cargo ship *Hestia*, meanwhile,

---

[73] Fritz Brustat-Naval, *Unternehmen Rettung*, (Hamburg, 2001), p. 240.

made 14 crossings carrying a total of over 30,000 evacuees.[74]

For all the logistical brilliance and the bravery of the seamen involved, modern scholarship has rather taken the shine off "Operation Hannibal" by revising the numbers involved downwards to around 1 million, and by bringing the proclaimed humanitarian rationale behind the effort into question.[75] Late in his life, long after his release from Spandau, Grand Admiral Karl Dönitz – Hitler's anointed successor and the former commander-in-chief of the German Navy – would claim that the evacuation from East Prussia in 1945 had been a "service to humanity"; "We did what we could in the circumstances", he wrote, "to save

---

[74] Ibid., p. 241.
[75] See, for instance, Schwendemann, op. cit.

the German population".[76] However, Dönitz's recollections in this regard were a little wide of the mark. Certainly large numbers of Germans were saved from the advance of the Red Army, but the primary rationale behind the operation was mainly military rather than humanitarian.

It goes without saying that Karl Dönitz was no woolly liberal. He was a Nazi believer, an impassioned follower of Adolf Hitler, who in 1944 called for all German soldiers to "fight fanatically" and to "stand fanatically behind the National Socialist state." His priority in the spring of 1945 was not the evacuation of German civilians threatened by the Soviet advance, it was the maintenance and preservation of the remaining German ports in the eastern Baltic: Pillau, Gotenhafen and Danzig, in the "fanatical" belief that German

---

[76] Quoted in Brustat-Naval, op. cit., pp. 232-3.

positions on land could thereby be held and that the newly-developed Type XXI U-boat might be able to defeat the Red Navy in the Baltic. It was for this purpose that the entire Baltic fleet – including the *Wilhelm Gustloff* – was subordinated to the military in January 1945. Munitions, fuel and supplies were to be ferried eastward, while the wounded would be evacuated westwards. The percentages foreseen by the German Navy allotted 40% for the transport of the wounded and 40% for military purposes. Only 20% was to be given over – and only where space allowed – for the evacuation of refugees.[77] Though these proportions would slip considerably as the needs of the civilians grew increasingly desperate, it should be clear that, in intention at

---

[77] Schwendemann, op. cit., p.3.

least, Dönitz's "service to humanity" was really nothing of the sort.

So it was that the first convoys of ships were prepared for departure. On January 25th the liners *Pretoria*, *Ubena* and *Duala* left Pillau in a snowstorm bound for Stettin; alongside them was the sister ship of the *Wilhelm Gustloff*, the *Robert Ley*, which, after making a stop at Gotenhafen, was laden with some 8,000 civilians and wounded. An eye-witness on the *Pretoria* recalled that, below decks, the vessel was packed so tightly there was no room for the evacuees to lie down. Their journey took five days.[78]

The *Gustloff* was also being readied. It was no easy task. After 4 years at the quayside as a floating barracks, she was scarcely seaworthy. Engines had to be serviced, drive trains

---

[78] Brustat-Naval, op. cit., p. 25.

overhauled, decks repaired. In addition, preparations had to be made for the accommodation of perhaps four times the usual number of passengers; restaurants and mess halls were cleared of tables and chairs, food and provisions were brought on board. Preparations were not helped by the curious fact that command of the *Gustloff* was divided between two captains. Not only was the commander of 2nd U-Boat Training Division, Wilhelm Zahn, still nominally in charge of his once barracks-ship, but the *Gustloff*'s pre-war merchant naval captain, the 67-year-old Friedrich Petersen, also retained command. Peculiarly, Petersen had been captured by the British earlier in the war but had been released on the grounds of his advanced age, and on the condition that he did not captain another ship. Returning to captain the immobile, quay-bound

Gustloff in 1944 must have seemed a perfect compromise, except that now, he was preparing to take her to sea once again. Unaware of such complexities, the ship's crew, consisting of a core of German sailors augmented by Croat and other foreign auxiliaries, worked feverishly to bring the vessel up to scratch. As one of them recalled, "in the forty-eight hours [after the order was given] we didn't even have time to smoke a cigarette."[79]

All the while, conditions beyond the quayside continued to deteriorate. Beyond Gotenhafen, the East Prussian regional centre of Elbing – barely 50 miles away– was already under Soviet siege. Alarmingly for the German command, the Red Army had bypassed the East Prussian heartland and encircled the

---

[79] Walter Knust, quoted in Christopher Dobson, John Miller & Ronald Payne, *Die Versenkung der "Wilhelm Gustloff"*, (Munich, 1979), p. 57.

defenders to the west – leaving the so-called 'Heilingenbeil cauldron' in its wake – and was now bearing down the course of the lower Vistula towards Danzig and Gotenhafen. The attack on Elbing had been so swift and unexpected that Soviet tanks had rumbled into the town alongside the trams and traffic, scattering the terrified inhabitants and stopping only to fire into prominent buildings.[80] Though they were repulsed, their presence was a profound shock to all those who had previously considered that the front was still some distance away.

In Gotenhafen and nearby Danzig, conditions deteriorated with each passing day, as fresh groups of desperate refugees arrived from the east, all seeking to escape the onrushing

---

[80] Christopher Duffy, *Red Storm on the Reich: The Soviet March on Germany, 1945*, (London, 1991), p. 171.

Soviets. Quickly, the quayside at Gotenhafen was transformed into an apocalyptic scene, with the hordes of desperate refugees milling around in the snow alongside abandoned prams, trolleys and carts, many of the latter still piled high with their owners' few belongings. As one eyewitness recalled, some of the discarded possessions were rather more personal: "I remember the horses and dogs most clearly. They had carried and accompanied their owners on their journey but now they were abandoned as there was no food for them. They were everywhere; in the city centre and in the port."[81]

For many of the refugees, the *Wilhelm Gustloff* still had its pre-war aura of excellence and efficiency, an aura now overlaid with a more urgent desire for escape. The liner

---

[81] Quoted in Dobson, Miller & Payne, op. cit., p. 64.

became almost the physical embodiment of their salvation; a ticket out of a looming Hades. One eye-witness recalled that the huge shape of the *Gustloff* was "like Noah's Ark, with everyone streaming towards the gangplank."[82] Yet, for all the tens of thousands demanding access, the ship was initially only permitted to allow 4,000 of them to board. In the chaotic circumstances that followed, the authorities sought to maintain order as best they could, organising a ticketing system to prioritise deserving cases. And, on the evening of January 25th, the first 'passengers' – predominantly wounded military personnel –

---

[82] Winfried Harthun, quoted in Clemens Höges, Cordula Meyer, Erich Wiedemann & Klaus Wiegrefe, "Die verdrängte Tragödie", in Stefan Aust & Stephan Burgdorff (eds), *Die Flucht*, (Bonn, 2003), p. 57.

were brought aboard.[83] The first of the refugees followed soon after.

Such was the crush on the quayside that some of the passengers were obliged, literally, to fight their way through the masses to reach the ship. Papers were checked – once, twice – and they were shown, not to a cabin, but more often to one of the *Gustloff*'s open spaces; a former restaurant, a cinema or a mess hall, where mattresses were laid out. As one passenger recalled, "the ship was packed to the gunnels, with people packed together like sardines."[84] Every space in the ship was utilised. A group of 372 female naval auxiliaries were shown to E-deck, below the waterline, where they were allocated the former swimming pool, now

[83] Schön, *Katastrophe*, op. cit., pp. 197-200.
[84] Ursula Resas, quoted in Guido Knopp, *Der Untergang der 'Gustloff'*, (Munich, 2002), p. 54.

dry.[85] Even the luxuriously appointed "*Führer-cabin*", once reserved for Hitler himself, was given over to the 13-strong family of Gotenhafen's mayor, Horst Schlichting. Schlichting himself did not join them, citing his duty to defend his city; an experience that he would not survive.[86]

Once installed, passengers were given a life-vest and told to await a call to the mess hall where, by and by, some hot food would be served for the new arrivals. Considering the desperate straits in which Germany found itself in the spring of 1945, the *Gustloff* was remarkably well equipped and supplied. There was a medical station, which – though improvised – was nonetheless staffed with trained personnel and able to handle most

---

[85] Dobson, Miller & Payne, op. cit., p. 62.
[86] Schön, *Katastrophe*, op. cit., p. 229.

eventualities; including, it is thought, four births.[87]

The ship's kitchens were well also stocked, with as many as 60 half pig carcasses, as well as huge quantities of sugar, flour, potatoes, milk powder and bread, and so were able to maintain an almost continuous supply of food, including, most memorably for the passengers, pea soup and *Eintopf* stew.[88] One area in which the ship was less well-provisioned, however, was that of life boats. Shortly before her departure, it was discovered that the *Wilhelm Gustloff* possessed only 12 of her original 22 lifeboats, the others having been loaned or given to the military for use as floating batteries, and even those that were still in place were full of ice, with their davits frozen solid.

---

[87] Knopp, op, cit., p. 88.
[88] Ibid., pp. 55, 56.

Fortunately, enterprising crew members managed to source 18 smaller lifeboats from the environs of Gotenhafen, as well as a quantity of rescue floats, all of which were lashed to the sundeck in readiness.[89] Despite such efforts, however, it was abundantly clear that only a fraction of the *Gustloff*'s passengers could be accommodated in the event that the ship had to be abandoned.

Oblivious to such concerns, children excitedly explored the vessel's many decks and gangways. One of them, 16-year old Eva Luck, got lost and recalled in her diary how she was guided back to her mother by a friendly officer: "It was a shame that Daddy couldn't come with us", she wrote, "Otherwise I would have liked it. I've never been on a big ship."[90] Like the

---

[89] Dobson, Miller & Payne, op. cit., pp. 66, 69-70.
[90] Eva Luck, quoted in ibid., p. 67.

mayor, her father, being of military age, had been obliged to remain behind to defend Gotenhafen.

After three chaotic days of loading supplies and boarding passengers, on the 28th January an overcrowded *Wilhelm Gustloff* was ordered to take still more refugees, in addition to the 4,000 already accommodated. Among them was a young mother who had waited for the entire day on the freezing quayside with her parents and two small children, torturing herself with the thought that her husband was away at the front and she had had no opportunity to inform him of their departure. When she finally boarded the *Gustloff*, shortly after 10pm that night, she was shocked to be asked by an official for details of her next of kin; those to be informed in the event of any accident. Seeing her surprise, the official sought to calm her down: "don't worry", he said, "it's just a formality".[91]

Over the following forty-eight hours, in the frenzy to take aboard as many people as possible, the system of ticketing and registering the passengers was abandoned altogether. A further transport of wounded arrived, followed by another. Then the crew of the *Gustloff* were ordered to open the doors, particularly to women and children, taking in countless more refugees who were thronging the snowy quayside and growing increasingly desperate. By 5 o'clock on the evening of the 29th January, just short of 8,000 refugees had been counted onto the *Gustloff*, although only 5,000 of them were named. That total would increase still further as the night went on. It has been calculated that, by the time of her departure,

[91] Schön, *Katastrophe*, op. cit., pp. 224-5.

the *Wilhelm Gustloff* was carrying over 10,000 passengers.[92] After much prevarication, it was decided that night that the *Gustloff* would set sail for Stettin at twelve noon the following day – 30th January 1945.

One last formality had to be carried out. At 10.40am on the morning of departure, the *Gustloff* was boarded by a detachment of military police – the much-feared, so-called *Kettenhunde*, or 'chained dogs' – who were responsible for security behind the lines, and increasingly, for the capture of deserters. Soon after, over the tannoy, all males of military age – those between 15 and 60 years of age – were requested to muster on the upper deck, while the remainder of the ship was thoroughly searched. After then checking the papers of those gathered on the upper deck –

[92] Figures discussed in ibid., p. 11.

predominantly the injured and otherwise militarily superfluous – the military police left empty-handed. According to an eye-witness, they gave the impression of merely going through the motions; being seen to do their duty, however futile it might be.[93] With that, the vessel was cleared for departure.

At the allotted time, the *Gustloff* slipped her moorings and was gently nuzzled by four tugs out towards the Bay of Danzig. Behind her she left a mass of disappointed, desperate refugees – still thronging the quay amid the strewn detritus of those that had already boarded – who had to console themselves with the thought that they might find a berth on another ship to take them westward. Teenager, Charlotte Kuhn, recalled her family's disappointment that the *Gustloff* had "left

---

[93] Ibid., p. 235.

without them", and noted that their alternative was a "grey and ugly coal freighter", which made them all apprehensive.[94] As if to compound their frustration, while the *Gustloff* was still well within sight of the harbour, another refugee ship – the *Reval*, newly arrived from Pillau – drew alongside her and disgorged an additional 500 or so refugees, who clambered aboard via cargo nets and rope ladders.[95]

Then, in a gathering blizzard, the *Gustloff* set off north-eastward toward the mouth of the bay and the Hela peninsula, where she would turn north-west. Conditions were not good. As well as the snow, she would have to deal with a force-6 north-westerly, an air temperature of around 4° below freezing, and a visual range of

---

[94] Quoted in Walter Kempowski, *Das Echolot: Fuga Furiosa*, Vol. 3, (Munich, 2004), p. 200.
[95] Knopp, op. cit., pp. 64-5.

less than 3 miles. She made course, at a leisurely 12 knots, out into the main navigation channel, ignoring the order to undertake a defensive tack and – initially at least – sailing with her navigation lights illuminated.[96] She had only one escort vessel, the modest torpedo boat *Löwe*; a situation which one of her crew described as "a dog leading a giant into the night".[97] Given that the *Löwe*'s vital hydrophone equipment was malfunctioning, one might add that the 'dog' was half blind.

The ship's two captains, Zahn and Petersen, had quarrelled about the route the *Gustloff* was to take and the manner of her sailing. Zahn, the military commander, was perhaps more acutely aware of the threat that they faced and so had advocated following the Pomeranian shoreline,

[96] Brustat-Naval, op. cit., pp. 40-41.
[97] Wilhelm Zahn quoted in "Die verdrängte Tragödie", *Der Spiegel Special*, (2/2002), p. 35.

and sailing as fast as possible, in blackout conditions. Petersen, meanwhile, was mindful that the years of mothballing might have taken their toll on the ship, and so preferred to maintain a steady, slower pace, in the – as he saw it – safety of the main, deep water shipping lane, which ran around 20 miles off-shore. Petersen had prevailed.

As darkness fell that evening, there was lingering concern on board, certainly, but also a quiet jubilation; a belief among many of the passengers that setting sail on the *Gustloff* marked the end of their tribulations. Passenger, Paul Uschdraweit, summed up the scene:

"There were about 300 people in the room, a few men, otherwise women and children of all ages. Their faces were careworn, often scarred by chilblains or secret tears, and in some of the mothers one saw the joy and the hope that now finally the terrible experiences of the last few days were over and this huge proud ship would take them and their children away from the horror."[98]

If any of the passengers had imagined for a moment that their ship was not at risk of attack, however, then they were grievously mistaken. The *Gustloff* was carrying large numbers of women and children – an absolute majority of those aboard – but she was not marked as a hospital ship and was also carrying military personnel, including many wounded and most of the 2nd U-boat Training Division. In addition, she had been armed, with three light anti-aircraft guns having been mounted to her

---

[98] Paul Uschdraweit, quoted in Kempowski, op. cit., p. 108.

bow, upper deck and aft sundeck.[99] She was a legitimate military target.

Consequently, the passengers were bombarded with orders and restrictions, via tannoy; banning the use of torches, for instance, or portable radios, either of which might possibly betray the ship's position to an unseen enemy. A further order followed, obliging all passengers to wear their life-vests at all times.[100] Clearly the *Gustloff*'s crew were under few illusions about the risk that they still faced.

As the *Wilhelm Gustloff* steamed westward into the gathering gloom of a Baltic snowstorm, her nemesis was lurking in the darkness of the deep. *S-13* was a Soviet attack submarine of the 'Stalinets' class. Eighty

---

[99] Wolfgang Müller, *30 Januar 1945: Die Untergang der "Wilhelm Gustloff"*, (Martenshagen, 2008), p. 13.
[100] Uschdraweit in Kempowski, op. cit., p. 110.

metres in length and with a displacement of around 900 tonnes, she was marginally larger and heavier than her German counterpart, the Type-VII, with which the U-boatmen aboard the *Gustloff* were so familiar. In fact, the S-class and the Type-VII had many similarities, and even shared some technological DNA; both being the end-product of a short-lived German/Soviet/Spanish collaboration from the early 1930's. With excellent manoeuvrability, the S-class was the most successful of all Soviet submarines of the Second World War.

S-13 had, thus far, had a less than illustrious career. She had been commissioned in the Baltic fleet during the fateful summer of 1941, just as Hitler's troops were overrunning the western Soviet Union. But, given the overwhelming dominance of German forces in that opening period – not least the many anti-submarine measures placed in the Gulf of Finland – she had been obliged to wait until the autumn of 1942 for her first successes: torpedoing the Finnish freighters *Hera* and *Jussi H*, and sinking the German ship *Anna W* in the Gulf of Bothnia. That mission might have proved *S-13*'s last when, returning towards her base at Moshchny Island, she was intercepted by two Finnish patrol boats, and forced into a crash dive which damaged her rudder after a heavy impact with the sea floor. Nonetheless, she managed to evade her pursuers and found her way to the Soviet naval base at Kronstadt, where she was repaired and relaunched in the spring of 1943, under a new commander; Alexander Marinesko.

Marinesko was well-regarded by his superiors. Born in Odessa in 1913, the son of a Romanian sailor, he had spent his entire adult life at sea, first in the Soviet merchant marine and then the Red Navy. His appointment to the command of *S-13* – one of the most advanced submarines in the Soviet fleet – was an expression of confidence both in his abilities and in his political reliability. However, by the turn of 1944-45, Marinesko was courting trouble. Not only had he failed to meaningfully engage the enemy for too many months, he was seemingly allowing the stress of his predicament to cloud his judgment. At New Year, while ashore in the Soviet naval base at Hanko, Marinesko found himself enamoured of the charms of a Swedish restaurant owner, and spent the following few days cavorting with the woman in a drunken stupor, absent without leave. When he finally reappeared aboard *S-13*, therefore, he was facing a court martial, not only for his unauthorised absence, but also for having fraternised with a non-Soviet citizen. Ordinarily, he might have expected a spell of hard labour in the gulag, or worse if his actions were interpreted as desertion. However, in the urgent circumstances of the hour, with the denouement drawing near in Germany's eastern provinces, and with his crew threatening not to sail without him, it was decided to postpone any decision on his fate.[101] *S-13* was belatedly sent out on patrol on the 11th January.

Both Marinesko and *S-13* therefore, had something to prove – both had reputations to redeem. They would soon get their chance. On the afternoon of January 30th, he and his crew were patrolling, undetected by the Germans, off the Bay of Danzig, eager to engage one of the vessels that they knew were evacuating

---

[101] Knopp, op. cit., p. 66.

men and materiel westwards from East Prussia. The mood on board was tense, expectant. One officer remembered that they had been on patrol for 20 days already and had thus far found anything. "We hadn't fired a shot", he wrote, "but now we had the feeling that we were where we had to be. We knew that a decision had to come, for better or for worse. Either we would find something, or something would find us. We were excited and ready for action."[102] At around 7pm that evening, they finally made contact. Watch officer Anatoli Vinogradov reported seeing lights towards the coast. At first, Marinesko and his officers discussed whether the lights might have been those of the German position at Hela, or at Rixhöft, but in due course radio operator Ivan Schnabzev received confirmation via

---

[102] Quoted in Dobson, Miller & Payne, op. cit., p. 100.

hydrophone: "I could hear the sound of twin screws", he recalled, "so the vessel before us had to be very big."[103] Marinesko then got the visual proof he needed:

"Suddenly I saw the silhouette of an ocean liner. It was huge. It even had its lights illuminated. I was immediately sure that it had to be 20,000 tonnes, certainly no less. I was also sure that it was packed with men who had trampled the earth of Mother Russia and were now attempting to flee. The vessel had to be sunk, I decided, and *S-13* would do it."[104]

After further observation confirmed the presence of an accompanying vessel – the *Löwe* – shadowing the *Gustloff* to the starboard side, Marinesko decided on a bold course of action. Though Soviet naval guidelines advised

---

[103] Knopp, op. cit., p. 74.
[104] Marinesko quoted in Dobson, Miller & Payne, op. cit., p. 105.

that submarines attack from a submerged position, so as to better exploit the element of concealment, Marinesko had other ideas. As a student of the methods of his enemy, he was keen to attack from the surface; in the manner of some of the most successful of Hitler's U-boat aces; 'decks awash', whereby he could more clearly observe his target and witness its demise. In addition, though he ran the constant danger of encountering mines, he opted to come around the *Gustloff* so as to be able to attack from her landward side, where *S-13* would not only evade the attentions of the *Löwe*, but would also be virtually invisible against the blackness of the Pomeranian coast.[105]

So it was, that Marinesko spent almost two hours overtaking the *Gustloff* and the *Löwe*

---

[105] Ibid., p. 103-5.

before closing in on the convoy from the port side. He was surprised, not only that he had not been discovered, despite spending all that time on the surface, but also that the *Gustloff* still had her navigation lights illuminated and that she was not following the evasive zig-zag course that he might have expected. Nonetheless, as he closed to a range of around 1,000 metres, located just off the shallows of the Stolpe Bank, he ordered that *S-13*'s four bow torpedo tubes be flooded and readied for firing at a depth of 3 metres. As was usual, the torpedoes themselves had been decorated with Soviet mottos: number 1 bore the message "For the Motherland!", number 2 proclaimed "For Stalin!", number 3 '"For the Soviet people!" and number 4 "For Leningrad!". For Marinesko and his crew, this was nothing more than an act of revenge. At 9.09pm, local time, at a distance of around 500 metres, he gave the order to fire.[106]

Aboard the *Wilhelm Gustloff*, the mood was mixed. The initial optimism and enthusiasm that had accompanied her long-awaited departure had paled once the harsh realities of a wintertime sea journey had dawned. Seasickness was very common, and given the crush aboard, very few sufferers were able to reach a toilet or an outside handrail. There was another reason for nausea. The 30th of January was the twelfth anniversary of Hitler's "seizure of power"; one of the red-letter days of the Nazi calendar. Hitler made a public speech – a rare occurrence by that stage in the war – which was relayed via radio aboard ship. It was vintage Hitler: unrepentant, unapologetic and defiant. He claimed that Nazi Germany had

---

[106] Ibid., p. 108.

achieved "tremendous things" and that the "impotent democracies" had attacked Germany out of "jealousy". Addressing the situation in the east, he promised that "the grim fate playing itself out in the villages, the market squares and on the land will be mastered and reversed." He then instructed his listeners to "fear nothing" and to obey his command to resist. He finished, rather ominously, by invoking the 'martyrs' of the Nazi movement:

"I appeal in this hour to the entire German people, but first and foremost to my old comrades and to all soldiers – to steel themselves with a still greater, harder spirit of resistance, until we – just as before – can engrave upon the tombs of the dead of this tumultuous struggle, the legend 'And yet you were victorious'."[107]

A few Nazi stalwarts might have approved, but for many of those aboard, Hitler's voice was the last they wanted to hear. Helga Reuter remembered doing her level best to ignore the speech.[108]

As the speech drew to a close, and the last bars of "*Deutschland, Deutschland über Alles*" faded, the two captains – Wilhelm Zahn and Friedrich Petersen – were on the bridge cautiously congratulating themselves with a cognac toast, believing that they had successfully negotiated the most threatening part of the journey. They were discussing the

---

[107] Text of the speech reproduced in *Völkischer Beobachter*, 1 February 1945, p. 1.
[108] Quoted in Cathryn Prince, *Death in the Baltic*, (Basingstoke, 2013), p. 131.

idea of increasing the *Gustloff*'s speed, when the first of *S-13*'s torpedoes struck.

The first impact struck the bow, directly below the bridge. For many of the survivors, the sound of that first detonation was something that would remain with them. It was, one of them recalled, "a deafening crash, a loud, shrill splintering sound, as though a glass wardrobe had been tipped over."[109] Ripped from their slumbers, many passengers momentarily concluded that the *Gustloff* must have hit a mine, but then the second impact followed – striking the forward quarter of the ship, in the area of the swimming pool – then the third, exploding amidships, knocking out the engine room.[110] The few that still had their

---

[109] Knopp, op. cit., p. 91.
[110] Schön, op. cit., front endpapers.

wits about them would have realised that their ship had been hit by torpedoes.

On the bridge, the officers noted that – almost immediately – the *Gustloff* took on a 5° list to port and the bow dipped downwards, testament to the damage that had been wrought below the waterline. The order was given for the engines to stop – a wholly superfluous measure, given that the engine room had been fatally compromised by the third impact. The ship was already in darkness, having lost power, and would shortly be illuminated only by gloomy emergency lighting. In the meantime, one of the officers told his men to fire off every flare they could find, bathing the stricken vessel in an eerie blood red light.[111] Another attempted to send out a frantic mayday, announcing:

---

[111] Prince, op. cit., p. 137.

"*Wilhelm Gustloff* sinking. Position: Stolpmünde –55° 07' North; 17° 42' East. Request assistance."

However, with the main power knocked out, he was forced to use an emergency transmitter with only limited range. It was highly doubtful that anyone beyond the nearby *Löwe* could hear him. A second order then went out from the bridge, demanding that the bulkheads, which might seal off those parts of the vessel that were already flooding, were to be closed. A third – as seemingly superfluous as the others – informed all passengers to make their way to the upper decks and reminded them not to panic.

Sadly, panic was already rife aboard the *Gustloff*. The chaos and screaming that had accompanied the first torpedo impact did not abate, and grew with each passing minute as the icy Baltic water flooded in and the ship began to list. In her cabin below deck, 17-year old Gertrud Agnesons witnessed the panic at first hand. As she tried desperately to light a match in the gloom, she spotted one of her fellows, lying wide-eyed and motionless in her hammock, clutching a torch in her hands. She seemed to have lost the ability to move. As the water began to stream into the cabin, Gertrud wrenched the torch from her grip and left the girl to her fate.[112]

As if to compound the catastrophe that was unfolding below deck, the U-boat crewmen aboard – who knew the ship's layout well and would have been essential for any orderly evacuation – had been billeted in the forward section that had been hit by the first torpedo. Those that survived the impact were then

---

[112] Quoted in Dobson, Miller & Payne, op. cit., p.123.

sacrificed by the captain's order to seal the forward bulkheads, in a desperate effort to buy more time for the ship. They, too, were left to their fate. Some eye-witnesses recalled hearing pistol shots from behind the sealed bulkhead doors, presumably as those trapped ended their lives before they drowned.[113]

Some of the most harrowing scenes were played out in the area of the swimming pool, where nearly 400 young, female naval auxiliaries had been accommodated; many of them in the empty pool itself. When the second torpedo hit, just below the swimming pool, the area was immediately compromised, with freezing seawater rushing in to engulf the unfortunates within. Within minutes, the pool area was transformed into a hideous, seething mass of corpses, personal effects and fractured

---

[113] Ibid., p. 126.

masonry. As one eye-witness recalled, it was a horrific scene:

"My comrades were everywhere, some already under water; a screaming, praying mass. The girls who were not yet dead or drowned were trying to climb the stairs to get out, but the doors were sealed, there was no escape... I heard screams for their mothers, for God; for help... A girl next to me had a knife from somewhere and slit her wrists – her blood mixed with the water, rising ever higher."[114]

Only two of the 372 marine auxiliaries who had been sleeping there would survive the night.[115] Over 200 of them – from Anna Faust to Rosa Zehe – would be listed as missing;[116] suggesting that many never even escaped the confines of the swimming pool.

---

[114] Ursula Pautz, quoted in *Spiegel*, op. cit., p. 30.
[115] Knopp, op. cit., p. 93.
[116] Missing are listed in Schön, op. cit., pp. 469-478.

For those that did make it to the stairwells, further murderous chaos ensued. Within minutes of the torpedo impacts, the *Gustloff* had listed 30° to port, making even unhurried progress around the vessel extremely difficult; walls became floors, and stairs quickly became impassable. One survivor recalled that the angle of the ship meant that women, children and the elderly had practically no chance of escape. "Because of the list, stairwells became so steep that only the strong could get up them, those that could pull themselves up. Some soldiers tried to help people up with ropes, but it didn't work."[117] There were other perils. In the music room, a grand piano succumbed to gravity and broke its moorings; careening across the hall, scattering women and children – and crushing the unfortunate – it smashed

---

[117] Quoted in Knopp, op. cit., p. 102.

itself to matchwood against the port flank of the ship with a cacophonous din.[118]

Such difficulties only fed the panic, and in the resulting crush to make it to safety, many were consumed by a brutal survival instinct which gave no quarter to their fellow passengers. U-boatman Heinz-Günther Bertram witnessed the horrific spectacle: "Everywhere there were open cases, bags were flung around; there were children there, children squashed flat. I saw a baby in a wicker basket, it was bleeding and had stopped moving. The people just climbed over it." "If you fell", he added, "you were lost".[119] Milda Bendrich was one of those trying to escape the carnage. Carrying her daughter Inge in her arms, she clambered over a heap of bodies, crushed by the stampeding

---

[118] Dobson, Miller & Payne, op. cit., p. 134.
[119] Knopp, op. cit., p. 96.

feet, littering the doorways and the stairwells, as she headed onwards towards the dim red glow that shone above.[120] Most of the dead had been crushed in the mêlée, but a few – it seems – had merely given up the struggle and had simply sat down on the steps to await death. One survivor recalled hearing a mother in the darkness, calmly telling her children that it was "time to die."[121] Hundreds must have met their fate in this way, without ever leaving the ship.

Another gruesome pinch-point for those trying to escape the *Gustloff* was the Lower Promenade Deck, which appeared to hold the promise of salvation but – completely enclosed, with toughened glass panels on both walls – was actually a deadly trap. Numerous eye-witness accounts tell of the hordes of

[120] Prince, op. cit., pp. 133-4.
[121] Ibid., p. 135.

desperate passengers filling the Promenade Deck, then realising that there was no escape but being unable to move back against the human tide. In desperation, as the waters rose towards them, the doomed passengers – whom one eye-witness described as "trapped like fish in an aquarium"[122] – tried to smash the glass, using their shoes, or anything else they could find. Officers fired their pistols at the toughened panes, to little effect. Heinz-Günther Bertram recalled with horror how "the ship sank lower and lower. I could see the people behind the glass, gasping for air, as the waters rose. They were caught in a glass coffin."[123]

For those who reached the upper promenade deck, the outlook was scarcely rosier. There, the provision of lifeboats and floats was

---

[122] Quoted in ibid., p. 135.
[123] Quoted in Knopp, op. cit., p. 102.

already woefully inadequate – despite the gallant efforts of the crew before the departure from Gotenhafen – and was now further diminished by circumstances, incompetence and neglect. The *Gustloff*'s heavy list to port, for instance, made launching any lifeboats on the starboard side of the vessel all but impossible, and to compound matters, many of the floats that had been lashed to the sundeck were frozen solid and could not be freed. Even on the port side there were problems. The lack of trained crewmen caused chaos: one sailor would later recall that "nothing was prepared. No-one had shown us how to operate the winches."[124] Furthermore, lifeboat davits, having lacked maintenance for many years, were often frozen or seized, and even when they worked were unreliable. One lifeboat had

---

[124] Ibid., p. 98.

jammed half-way through being lowered, and was swaying violently above the water until an enterprising passenger called out for a penknife to cut the frozen ropes. Finally released, the lifeboat crashed down to the surface but thankfully remained afloat, saving the lives of the 70 or so passengers aboard.[125] Others were not so lucky. A seized line caused one lifeboat to tip on its end, half-way through its descent, pitching its contents – mainly women and children – into the inky waters below. "They had no chance", said an eye-witness.[126] The *Gustloff*'s captain would later estimate that – at best – only 6 of the ship's lifeboats were successfully launched.[127]

Unsurprisingly, in the chaos of the sinking ship, discipline broke down almost entirely.

[125] Prince, op. cit., p. 138.
[126] Knopp, op. cit., p. 99.
[127] Prince, op. cit., p. 132.

The concept of 'Women and Children First' appears to have been honoured only in the breach. This seems to have applied not only among the ordinary passengers – where a brutal "devil take the hindmost" attitude reigned – but, more surprisingly, among many of the crew and military personnel. In one instance, a lifeboat designed for over 50 passengers was set afloat with only around a dozen sailors aboard, saving themselves while the women and children thronged the icy deck. Witnessing the scene, an officer could only shout "*Schweine!*"[128] Many survivors' accounts tell of desperate officers being forced to fire warning shots in an attempt to maintain order. They rarely succeeded.

In fact, it seems weapons were being used for very different purposes aboard the *Gustloff*.

---

[128] Dobson, Miller & Payne, op. cit., p. 124.

Caught between an overcrowded, sinking ship and certain death in the freezing waters of the Baltic, it is unsurprising that many passengers and crew opted to take their own lives. However, the high incidence of suicide on board the *Gustloff* was also an echo of the dark millenarianism that was already a grim feature of the dying days of the Third Reich; the belief that civilization itself was crumbling and the world that would succeed would not be worth living in.[129] There are numerous examples, with many survivors recalling hearing pistol shots or seeing muzzle flashes in the darkness. One remembered seeing a man in Nazi Party uniform, standing on the icy deck with his family. The man's wife shouted: "Come on! Finish it!" and he fired three shots before

---

[129] On this subject, see Christian Goeschel, *Suicide in the Third Reich*, (Oxford, 2009).

putting the gun to his temple. Then there was silence as the pistol jammed. In his frustration, the man turned around to ask for a replacement, but he lost his footing and slid down the deck; following his family into oblivion.[130] Others saw corpses with their wrists slit, or witnessed desperate passengers stripping naked before jumping into the freezing water, knowing that they would thus be granted a swifter death.[131] A crewman checking below deck recalled hearing a shot from behind a closed cabin door. Pushing the door open, he saw a woman and child dead on the floor, and an officer standing over them with a still-smoking pistol, a terrified 5-year old clinging to his legs. As he closed the door,

---

[130] Schön, op. cit., p. 330.
[131] See Aust & Burgdorff (eds), op. cit., p. 52 and Prince, op. cit., p. 139.

he realised, with horror, that he had interrupted a family suicide.[132]

In spite of the chaos enveloping them, almost all the survivors remember the moment that the *Gustloff* finally sank. By around 10.15pm, local time, an hour after the first torpedo had hit, the ship was already in her death throes. Listing now at an impossible angle, with the railing of her Promenade Deck being swept by each and every freezing wave, the *Gustloff* was doomed, and the last desperate passengers still crowding the deck began to drop into the waters below. Among them was the ship's 18-year old assistant purser, Heinz Schön, who had crawled onto one of the emergency rafts, still stowed on the *Gustloff*'s deck, in the hope that the rising

---

[132] Schön, op. cit., p. 304.

waters would carry him away to safety, which – fortunately for him – they did.[133]

Watching the *Gustloff*, witnesses recalled how she keeled over to almost 90°; her funnel now being lashed by the waves, before tilting forward, bow first. With that, she creaked and groaned, as the bulkheads fractured. Some report a dull crescendo of screams from the many hundreds of doomed passengers still aboard; a sound "so terrible", one survivor said, "that no-one who didn't hear it could describe". "It was the death cry of the *Gustloff*", another remembered, "I can hear it still."[134] There were other strange sounds to rend the night air. After spending much of the last hour in a sinister half-light, as the stricken vessel tipped forward, power was momentarily

---

[133] Ibid., p. 330.
[134] Quoted in Kempowski, op. cit., pp. 206-7 and Knopp, op. cit., p. 110.

restored and both the lights and the siren sprang back into life. "It was ghostly" said Heinz Schön, "the *Gustloff* went down fully lit, reflected a thousand times across a seething sea". At the same time "the siren announced the ship's demise. A long note filled the air, became quieter – hoarser [...] Then it spluttered out and the lights were extinguished."[135] With that, the *Wilhelm Gustloff* finally disappeared beneath the waves, taking with it the countless hundreds of passengers who had never reached the deck.

For those that were left, it was a desolate scene. In the pitch dark of a freezing Baltic night, they found themselves bobbing amid the assorted debris of thousands of human lives. A fortunate few were safe aboard a life-boat, including the *Gustloff*'s merchant captain

---

[135] Schön, op. cit., p. 336.

Friedrich Petersen; others clung desperately to life-rafts. The majority – dead and alive – simply floated. Some recalled seeing children tipped upside down by their life-vests; their heads below the surface, their legs splaying into the night air.[136] Others cried out for help, or – more usually – were stunned into an impotent silence by shock and the extreme cold, which gave them only minutes before they lapsed into unconsciousness. They would surface, again and again, eyes wide with terror, before sinking beneath the waves. Those faces, one eye-witness recalled, were unforgettable, even many years later: "Some of them are still so clear to me", she said, "that I could sketch them."[137]

---

[136] Quoted in Kempowski, op. cit., p. 207.
[137] Knopp, op. cit., p. 112.

Some endeavoured to save the drowning by pulling them onto their rafts, or into their life-boats. Few succeeded. Not only were all those concerned already physically exhausted by their ordeal, there were also concerns among those already aboard that such efforts might overload their refuge, or cause it to overturn. Ursula Birkle did her best to pull three survivors into her life-boat, but was deterred by her fellows who told her to stop; "we'll all drown" they said, "if more people come aboard." In another tragic case, a mother swam towards a life-boat lifting her child as best she could out of the water: "At least take my child!" she begged. But – numbed by the cold and the shock – nobody on board helped her.[138]

A gallant few, at least, were helping such unfortunates. The torpedo boat *Löwe*, which

[138] Both from ibid., pp. 110-111.

had escorted the *Gustloff* and had relayed her mayday message, was already taking survivors aboard, by lowering cargo nets to the waterline. Despite her comparatively small size – she was a former Norwegian vessel of only 70m in length – she saved 472 of *Gustloff*'s passengers, delivering them to the nearby port of Olberg later that night.[139] Just before the *Gustloff* sank, the *Löwe* was joined in the rescue effort by a second torpedo boat, the larger *T-36*, which had been escorting the heavy cruiser *Admiral Hipper* through those same perilous waters. The *Admiral Hipper* refused to assist – citing the threat of being torpedoed by the same submarine that had sunk the *Gustloff* – and continued her journey westward, much to the astonishment of the survivors. One recalled: "We saw how this

[139] Schön, op. cit., p. 445.

battleship sailed past us. The searchlights scanned the water close to us, and then disappeared again. Our brothers just left us there."[140]

In fact, the threat to the *Admiral Hipper* was not just theoretical. Marinesko's *S-13* was still in the vicinity and had been watching the grim fate of the *Gustloff* from a safe distance. *S-13* had problems of her own, however. One of the four torpedoes fired at the *Gustloff* – the one christened "For Stalin!" – had jammed in the tube and threatened to detonate at any time, so it had to be hurriedly disarmed before the submarine could continue its attack. That done, *S-13* was free to engage the enemy once again, and for a few minutes the *Admiral Hipper* offered a tantalising target, before hurriedly departing.

---

[140] Knopp, op. cit., p. 114.

The *T-36* did assist, however; motivated in part perhaps by the fact that her captain's mother had been aboard the *Gustloff* that night. It was a ticklish operation, though. For one thing, *T-36* was forced to manoeuvre amidst a mass of floating humanity and so risked maiming and killing the survivors with every turn of her propellers. In addition, she was already aware of the presence of *S-13* and so was forced to position herself bow-on to the submarine, so as to present as small a target as possible. At one point, she had to withdraw temporarily from the debris field, and, as she did so evaded two torpedoes fired from *S-13*. Responding with a round of depths charges, she drove off her foe, but in the process cannot have avoided killing some of the survivors she was trying to rescue. Others were blown from their floats into the freezing waters. One; Rudi

Lange, recalled: "I was frightened to death by the roar. With every explosion, I thought my eardrums would burst."[141] Nonetheless, he was one of the lucky ones.

Returning to their task, the crew of *T-36* lowered cargo nets into the water and launching their own life-boats, as they continued helping the exhausted passengers aboard. It was back-breaking work; many of the survivors were fully clothed and by now lacked the strength to help themselves, so were a dead weight for the *T-36*'s sailors. Some survivors were already beyond help, and succumbed to shock and hypothermia even in the moment of their salvation. Most, however, were rushed below deck where they were swiftly undressed, put under hot showers and then vigorously rubbed dry. Thereafter, they

[141] Dobson, Miller & Payne, op. cit., pp. 149.

were given dry clothes and revived with schnapps or hot tea. Hans-Joachim Elbrecht was one of those saved by *T-36*, and even with this treatment, it took him four hours to physically recover from his ordeal.[142] In all, *T-36* would deliver 564 survivors from the *Gustloff* to the port of Sassnitz on Rügen Island. Combining that total with those rescued by the *Löwe*, the two torpedo boats would account for over 80 percent of the *Gustloff*'s 1,252 survivors – including the mother of *T-36*'s captain.[143]

*

In the immediate aftermath of the sinking, the fate of the *Wilhelm Gustloff* was scarcely discussed. Given the dire straits in which Nazi Germany found itself in those last months of

---

[142] Knopp, op. cit., p. 117.
[143] Figures from Schön, op. cit., p. 445.

the war, with attacks on all fronts and deaths and casualties multiplying everywhere, this is perhaps unsurprising. But, it is nonetheless clear that news of the *Gustloff*'s sinking was suppressed. In official circles a number of dubious rumours circulated, not least amongst them that the *Gustloff* had merely beached on a sandbank with minimal casualties.[144] But the Nazi hierarchy were certainly not ignorant of the vessel's true fate. Goebbels wrote in his diary on 1st February 1945 that the ship had been lost, with "4,000 lives", and had most likely been torpedoed by the Soviets.[145] The German press, however – which would soon be reduced to producing single sheets of propaganda messages and pointless exhortations to resist – ignored the news.

---

[144] Quoted in Schön, op. cit., p. 418.
[145] Fröhlich (ed.), op. cit., Part II, Vol. XV, (Munich, 1995), p. 291.

In the circumstances, it was the foreign media that reported the *Gustloff*'s demise. Finnish radio was the first to break the news, followed by *The Times* of London, which reported on the 19th February 1945 that the vessel had been torpedoed "after leaving Danzig" and had sunk "within a few minutes". Two days later, the Swedish *Dagens Nyheter* carried the story, correctly estimating the number of passengers on board the vessel at around 10,000.[146] Despite the silence on the German Home Front, the story of the *Gustloff* spread, nonetheless, via the whispered accounts of survivors and eye-witnesses. In late February 1945, for instance, a secret 'mood report' by a Wehrmacht propaganda unit in Berlin listed the loss of the *Gustloff* "with 11,000 passengers

---

[146] Schön, op. cit., p. 407.

aboard" as one of a number of 'rumours' that were then doing the rounds.[147]

Those who saw the corpses stacked on the docksides at Pillau or Gotenhafen, or saw the bodies washing ashore along the Pomeranian coast, at Stolpmünde or Leba, would have known very well that the sinking of the *Wilhelm Gustloff* was no 'rumour'. Though records – if they were ever kept – are most likely lost, one must assume that many hundreds of corpses were found that spring and beyond. Only a few of them ever found a formal resting place. In the early days, bodies were taken to the market hall in Gotenhafen where the authorities sought as best they could to identify them. So it was, that 17 named bodies of naval personnel were buried in a

[147] Wolfram Wette, Ricarda Bremer & Detlef Vogel (eds), *Das letzte halbe Jahr*, (Essen, 2001), p. 253.

mass grave in the town in February 1945. A further 143 were buried (41 of them named) in a mass grave in a cemetery in Pillau.[148] However, these were but a tiny fraction of the total. And as the military situation deteriorated that spring, the efforts to recover and identify the dead collapsed entirely. With the arrival of the Soviets, most of those that were found were disposed of in hastily-dug mass graves all along the coast of Pomerania, particularly in the town cemetery at Stolpmünde.[149] Later, as the numbers washing ashore grew, they were buried in the dunes between Leba and Stolpmünde. As one eye-witness recalled: "all

---

[148] Schön, op. cit., pp. 483-5.
[149] Marcin Jamkowski, *Duchy z głębin Bałtyku: Steuben, Gustloff, Goya*, (Warsaw, 2010), p. 144.

those dead were nameless, no one knew them, no one wanted to know them."[150]

For most of the bereaved, therefore, there was nothing. There was no body, no burial, and for their families and loved ones, there was nothing but an empty silence. One example must serve to illuminate this wider story. Walter Salk was a 21-year old seaman-mechanic, attached to the 2nd U-boat Training Division in Gotenhafen. A dutiful son, he wrote regular letters to his parents in Essen, keeping them informed about his affairs. In his last letter, dated 14 January 1945, he said that he would be "glad to leave Gotenhafen", and that he would forward his new address when he

---

[150] Adolf Bohlman, quoted in "Wydymy w Ustce to wielki cmentarz ofiar z Gustloffa u Steubena – relacja swiadka" in *Głos Pomorza*, 9 February 2010 -
http://www.gp24.pl/wiadomosci/ustka/art/4443499,wydmy-w-ustce-to-wielki-cmentarz-ofiar-z-gustloffa-i-steubena-relacja-swiadka,id,t.html

had it. With that, he closed, as he had to go on duty. Walter's parents heard nothing more from him. Their letter to Gotenhafen, dated 1 February, was returned as undeliverable, and as they knew nothing about the sinking of the *Gustloff*, they were left totally in the dark. Then, five weeks later a letter from a friend of Walter's, Christa Hausen, seemed to shed some light on his fate. She asked if they knew anything about Walter's whereabouts and told them of her "dread" that he had been aboard the torpedoed *Gustloff*. In December 1945, he was officially listed as missing. Then, in September of the following year, he was legally declared dead by the British occupation authorities: "Your son was not one of the survivors to be rescued" the letter declared to his parents, "so you must reconcile yourself that he is no longer among the living [...]

Should you not have heard from your son by now, we officiate that he is legally declared dead and recorded as such in Hamburg."[151] Needless to say, Walter's body was never identified.

Many among the bereaved accepted that painful news with resignation, and an inevitable sense of guilt. Irmgard Harnecker was just 20-years old when she lost her two-year old daughter, Ingrid, aboard the *Gustloff*; the toddler swept from her mother's arms by a wave. Irmgard cursed herself for surviving, and the loss – and her own feelings of guilt – overshadowed the remainder of her life. "It is so long ago", she said in an interview in 2002, "but it still hurts"; adding that: "It will only

[151] The case of Walter Salk is at -
http://www.wilhelmgustloff.com/stories_victims_WSalk.htm
with thanks to Rita Rowand.

stop when I'm dead too".[152] Irmgard Harnecker died in December 2014.

There were countless other tragedies and dramas; surviving parents desperately seeking their lost children, and orphans forever unsure of whom they really are. As late as 1985, the Red Cross was listing unidentified children rescued from the *Gustloff* on its Tracing Service:

"Child Tracing Service – 2699 – female

Surname: unknown

First Name: unknown

Assumed date of birth: 1 November 1944

Found: Rescued from the sinking of the *Wilhelm Gustloff*, 30th January 1945

Clothing: swaddling wrap

Description: Blue eyes, mid-blonde hair."[153]

---

[152] Irmgard Harnecker, quoted in *Spiegel*, op. cit., p. 35.
[153] In Kempowski, op. cit., p. 216.

It is not known whether 'Child 2699' – who by then was a 40-year old woman – was ever claimed.

For many years after the war, Wolfgang Heye was convinced that his wife and two sons had been lost aboard the *Gustloff* – their names had been on the ship's manifest and they had not been among the survivors – so he had searched no further. By chance, however, he discovered his wife again in 1960. She had decided against travelling by sea from Gotenhafen that January, and had survived, along with her children. There was to be no happy ending, however, as both husband and wife had, by that time, remarried and begun new lives.[154]

Hermann Freymüller's story is altogether darker. He had personally escorted his wife, Elsa, and two children to the dockside by the

---

[154] Knopp, op. cit., pp. 60-61.

Gustloff in January 1945, in the hope and expectation that he would follow as soon as he could. When news of the sinking broke, however, and he was told that his wife and children were not among the rescued, he was nonetheless convinced that his baby son – 17-month old Frank-Michael – had survived the wreck. So began a lifelong quest to find the boy. At first, Freymüller made little headway, but in 1948 he was informed that a child matching Frank-Michael's description had been registered by the authorities in Rostock. The child in question had been rescued from the *Gustloff* sinking by his now-adoptive father, Werner Fick, and had been the only survivor in his lifeboat; tightly wrapped in a bundle of blankets. Assuming that the child's parents had perished, Fick – whose own marriage was childless – had decided then and there to adopt the infant, and in due course took him back to the family home and raised him as his own, christening him Peter.

Unsurprisingly, perhaps, Freymüller's subsequent and increasingly determined efforts to establish the true identity of 'Peter' were not welcomed in the Fick household. And the ensuing legal conundrum was further complicated by the fact that Freymüller now lived in the German Federal Republic, while the Fick family lived in the communist GDR. The resulting Gordian Knot became so intractable that, in 1952, Freymüller appealed to the highest offices in the land: GDR minister-president Otto Grotewohl, for assistance. Grotewohl's solution was as simple as it was – to Freymüller – unsatisfactory; he decreed that 'Peter' could decide for himself, when he reached the age of 21, whether or not he wanted to establish his true identity, and until that time, the case was closed. Sadly for Freymüller, he died in 1964, six months before Peter's 21st birthday, without ever meeting the young man he believed to be his son and without ever discovering the truth.[155]

The experience of another *Gustloff* 'orphan'; Heidrun Gloza, showed that such longed-for reunions – even when they succeeded – were not always joyous. She recalled that, though her childhood with her adoptive parents was a happy one, she constantly dreamt of her biological mother: "my thoughts were always with her", she said, "How did she look? Where did I belong? Who was I anyway?" Heidrun's dreams were seemingly answered in 1981

---

[155] On the Freymüller story, see *Focus* magazine, 28 February 2008, http://www.stern.de/politik/geschichte/-wilhelm-gustloff---seid-still--wir-muessen-alle-sterben--3083234.html and also Schön, op. cit., pp. 417-431.

when – courtesy of a distinctive mole – the Red Cross finding service finally reunited mother and daughter after 36 years apart. But the happy ending proved elusive. The relationship was strained and the two found that they had little to say to one another. Both had been chasing an ideal; a dream. Heidrun's mother confessed as much when she said that she had been "looking for a child and had found a fully-grown woman".[156] Even decades later, it seems, the *Wilhelm Gustloff* was still casting a long shadow.

Alexander Marinesko was another who never freed himself from the *Gustloff*. As the U-boat commander who had masterminded the vessel's sinking, he expected to be richly rewarded by the Soviet state, when he returned *S-13* from patrol in February 1945. As well as

[156] See *Focus* magazine, op. cit.

the *Gustloff*, he had also sunk a second luxury liner, the *General von Steuben*, at the cost of a further 4,000 lives, making him the most successful Soviet submarine commander of the war. Yet, he arrived back into port to a frosty reception, and when a new round of awards for naval personnel was then announced, he was angered to only receive the "Order of the Red Banner", instead of the highly prestigious "Hero of the Soviet Union". His anger was only heightened when he learnt that another submarine commander, Vladimir Konovalov, who had a lesser tally to his name, had been made a "Hero". Due to his earlier indiscretions, it appears, Marinesko was now a marked man with the Soviet secret police, the NKVD, and even his successes were not enough to salvage his blackened reputation. To add to his woes, he then wrote a critique of Soviet submarine tactics – somewhat unwisely – citing his experiences with the *Gustloff* as his justification. There was much to legitimately criticise, and such action would scarcely be considered controversial outside of the USSR, but combined with his disciplinary record, it was almost a counter-revolutionary act.[157]

After a last patrol in the Baltic that spring, during which the war came to an end, Marinesko was reduced to the ranks and given a dishonourable discharge from the Soviet Navy; accused of negligence, drunkenness and promiscuity, a reference to his unauthorised absence prior to sinking the *Gustloff*. Rejected from the merchant marine, he found work near Leningrad in a state depot for building materials. But the NKVD were watching his every move. And when he complained about

[157] Dobson, Miller & Payne, op. cit., pp. 192-4.

corruption at the depot in 1949, he was in turn accused of theft and given a three year sentence of hard labour in the infamous *Gulag* camp at Kolyma, inside the Soviet Arctic circle. Rehabilitated and released in 1955, during the 'thaw' that followed Stalin's death, Marinesko returned to Leningrad, and to a modicum of respectability; being restored to his previous rank and granted a pension. Now, at least he was no longer a 'non-person', but his health had been broken and he died of cancer in 1963, aged 50. Twenty-seven years later, in 1990, Marinesko finally received the recognition that he had craved in life. As one of the last such awards in its history, he was finally granted the title of "Hero of the Soviet Union" by Soviet premier, Mikhail Gorbachev.

Strangely, Marinesko's German counterparts fared little better. Though the sinking of the

Gustloff is history's worst maritime disaster, it was still – until the turn of the century at least – ignored within Germany and practically unknown without. This ignorance had everything to do with Germany's efforts to deal with its ignominious Nazi past – the process of *Vergangenheitsbewältigung*. Once it got into gear, from the 1960's onwards, this process tended to take the form of an ongoing confrontation with the Nazi era, which naturally tended to concentrate very firmly on German responsibility for the war and for the crimes of the Holocaust. In the resulting climate of "mea maxima culpa", instances of German victimhood in World War Two – whether they be the civilians suffering under Allied bombing, or indeed those unfortunates aboard the *Gustloff* – tended to find no place in the narrative. More than that, those who tried to tell such stories were suspected of harbouring right-wing, neo-Nazi tendencies – an accusation that tended to swiftly silence survivors and historians alike. Unsurprisingly then, the story of the *Wilhelm Gustloff* was gradually forgotten, and after a cinema retelling in 1960 in *Nacht fiel über Gotenhafen* ("Night fell over Gotenhafen"), it slipped from the public mind, seemingly for good.

So it was that many of those most closely associated with the story were also forgotten in Germany. The vessel's surviving captain, for instance; Wilhelm Zahn (Friedrich Petersen died soon after the end of the war), disappeared into obscurity. After testifying at a hearing in 1945, at which the extent of his own culpability in the disaster was not established, he left no further record. Despite an exemplary career as a U-boat commander, he never went back to sea and spent the remainder of his life as a salesman, dying in 1976. It is telling, perhaps, that neither Zahn nor Petersen appear to warrant an entry on German Wikipedia.

The fact that the story of the *Gustloff* was not forgotten altogether was down, largely, to the work of one man; Heinz Schön. Himself a survivor of the ship – upon which he had served as a young assistant purser – Schön wasted little time in the aftermath in seeking out survivors and collecting eye-witness testimony of the sinking, and quickly emerged as the leading authority on the subject. A number of publications followed – among them *Die Gustloff Katastrophe* – as well as an advisory role on the film *Nacht fiel über Gotenhafen*, but Schön was very much swimming against the current; trying to keep alive the memory of an event that most around him simply wanted to forget.

But that current would change, and Schön's dogged perseverance would pay off. After German reunification in 1990, a period of 'normalisation' ensued in the country's attitude to its own history; and slowly the taboo surrounding the thorny subject of German victimhood dissipated. The story of the *Wilhelm Gustloff* was soon finding a new audience, being written about in the news magazines and featuring on television documentaries; and Heinz Schön was in demand. He even featured in the seminal novel *Crabwalk* by Günter Grass – so often the guardian of Germany's conscience – in which the fate of the *Gustloff* was an essential part of the plot. In this way, the story of the *Wilhelm Gustloff*, long ignored and wished away, finally reached a worldwide audience and received the recognition that it warranted.

When Heinz Schön died in 2013, aged 86, his last wish was that his ashes should be scattered on the ship that he had spent most of his life studying. Accordingly, that summer, a team of six divers – three German and three Polish – placed his ashes on the wreck; contained in an urn made of rocksalt, which would slowly dissolve and so spread its contents across the site. Along with it, a plaque was left behind as a more permanent memorial, reading: "Rest in Peace. Heinz Schön. 1926-2013".[158] It was a sort of homecoming.

By the time that Schön's ashes were placed on the wreck, the *Gustloff* had been recognised as a war grave – but that had not always been

---

[158] See
http://www.nw.de/lokal/kreis_herford/herford/herford/8531611_Letzter_Wunsch_erfuellt.html

the case. Lying in around 40 metres of water, some 20 miles north of the port town of Łeba on the Polish coast, the wreck had long attracted the attentions of divers. The first were those of the Soviet government agency EPRON (ЭПРОН), who dived the vessel for three years between 1948 to 1951, using traditional diving equipment; heavy boots and spherical brass helmets. It has never been definitively established precisely what they were looking for, but they concentrated on the central section of the ship and used sophisticated cutting equipment and even explosives to cut away sections of the hull and decks.[159] The most sensible suspicion is that they were looking for documents; particularly blueprints for the advanced German Type XXI U-boats, which had been built at the Schichau

---

[159] Jamkowski, op. cit., p. 147-8.

Shipyard in Danzig before its dissolution in January 1945.[160]

Of course there are other, more imaginative, suggestions; including that they were looking for sensitive personnel documents, bank deposits, gold and jewellery, or samples of military technology. Some even maintain that the Soviet divers were looking for the famed Amber Room. Begun in Prussia around 1701 and gifted to the Russian Tsar, Peter the Great, in 1716, the Amber Room consisted of 6 tonnes of Baltic amber worked into decorative panels, covering – in its final form – 55 square metres. It was described by contemporaries as the eighth wonder of the world and was installed at Catherine Palace outside St

---

[160] See Piotr Olejarczyk *'Rekiny' zdobywają „Gustloffa" – z dziejów polskiego płetwonurkowania* at HistMag.org - http://histmag.org/Rekiny-zdobywaja-Gustloffa-z-dziejow-polskiego-pletwonurkowania-9058;1

Petersburg; the summer residence of the Russian Tsars. When German troops arrived in 1941, however, the Amber Room was boxed into 28 wooden crates and 'liberated'; being considered a prime example of Teutonic craftsmanship. Taken to Königsberg, it was put on display before being stored in 1944 due to the risk of damage from air raids. There it remained until January 1945, when – like much else in East Prussia – it was ordered to be removed westwards.

However, the Amber Room never arrived in the west, and since then its whereabouts have been the subject of fevered speculation and countless conspiracy theories. Most sensible perhaps, is the suggestion that the Amber Room – which was stored in the basement of the Royal Palace in Königsberg – was destroyed when the palace was burnt out in the

Soviet siege of 1945.[161] (Amber is fossilized tree resin and burns quite easily – its German name is *Bernstein*, a corruption of 'burn stone'). But there were other theories; that the Amber Room had been spirited westward and hidden, and – inevitably – that it had been put in the hold of the *Wilhelm Gustloff*; an idea spurred by eye-witnesses who dubiously claimed to have seen it being loaded aboard.[162]

Needless to say, the Amber Room was never recovered, and the Russian authorities are tight-lipped about the purpose of the Soviet dive, even to this day. What is clear, however, is that Soviet divers did immense damage to the wreck. Though the bow and stern are still largely intact, extensive cutting of the ship's

[161] See Catherine Scott-Clark & Adrian Levy, *The Amber Room: The Untold Story of the Greatest Hoax of the Twentieth Century*. (London, 2004).
[162] James Lucas, *Last Days of the Reich: The Collapse of Nazi Germany, May 1945*, (London, 2000), pp. 25-28.

hull has caused most of the mid-section to collapse in on itself, leaving it – as one expert noted – "hard to recognise as a naval vessel".[163]

Rumours about the Amber Room may well have spurred the Soviet dive mission on the *Gustloff* of the late 1940's, but they certainly played a role – albeit indirectly – in later Polish dives. As one dive veteran confessed, few Polish divers believed in the stories of the Amber Room being on board the vessel, but they exploited the possibility as a means of gaining funding and support for their expeditions.[164] The most thoroughgoing of these took place in 1973 and, as well as collating an inventory of the wreck, salvaged a few items, such as a propeller and the

---

[163] Jamkowski, op. cit., p. 148.
[164] Michał Rybicki, quoted in Olejarczyk, op. cit.

Gustloff's three anchors, all of which were later scrapped.[165] A second expedition was planned for 1980, but was abandoned due to the unstable political situation in Poland at that time.

As one of the largest wrecks in the Baltic, the *Gustloff* attracted continued interest from divers. It is considered to be a moderately challenging dive. Lying in relatively deep water for a scuba diver, at over 40 metres, there is no natural light and it is not always easy even to locate the vessel on the sea floor. Commercial diver Mike Fletcher recalled from his first dive on the site that:

"It took us many minutes just to find the wreck. And although I was prepared to find a wreck that didn't really resemble the *Gustloff*, I wasn't prepared for what I found. It was a mass

---

[165] Jamkowski, op. cit. p. 149.

of twisted and broken steel, nothing that resembled a ship. It took several minutes just to orientate ourselves; to know where we were, to try and get a sense of what was the stern and what was the bow."[166]

Part of the problem is the collapse of the ship's central section, which can easily disorientate a diver, and which now leaves only the stern accessible.[167] Moreover, even once a diver has found their bearings, the Baltic silt covering every surface is easily whipped into a fog, reducing visibility almost to zero. As one unfortunate noted, once the silt was disturbed on board, it was like "swimming through cream".[168] Physically and psychologically demanding, it is a wreck that can take an

---

[166] Wilhelm Gustloff: a Dive Commentary by Mike Fletcher, at https://www.youtube.com/watch?v=Zu2kiJiF_yM
[167] Author correspondence with dive veteran, Krzysztof Wnorowski.
[168] Rybicki in Olejarczyk, op. cit.

emotional toll, and has been described as "not unlike being in a graveyard at night." Perhaps for this reason, one Polish veteran said, with only a whiff of hyperbole, that: "what Mount Everest is for mountaineers, the *Gustloff* is for divers."[169]

Over the years, some divers have taken more than memories and have looted the vessel for 'mementos' – everything from wash basins to chandeliers – which have subsequently found their way into private collections. A porthole, raised in 1988, is currently exhibited at the German Naval Memorial at Laboe, near Kiel, for example, and in 2006, the ship's bell was the highlight of a history exhibition in New York.[170] It was a practice that was not without

---

[169] Mike Fletcher, op. cit., and Janusz Szczukowski, quoted in Olejarczyk, op. cit.
[170] Mark Landler, "Poles riled by Berlin exhibition" in Herald Tribune, August 30, 2006.

its perils. One diver rescued what – in the murky gloom of the wreck – he thought was a case of champagne, only to realise when he reached the surface that he had found a box of mortar bombs.[171] Nonetheless, the result is that the *Gustloff* has been effectively picked clean. As numerous divers report, there are very few personal effects and artefacts, and no human remains to be seen; hardly anything in fact to remind one of what it once was.

Such pilfering was belatedly halted in 2006, when the Polish Maritime Authority in Gdańsk declared the *Wilhelm Gustloff* to be a war grave, and forbade diving within 500 metres of the wreck. Those that transgress now face a

---

http://web.archive.org/web/20151124072931/http://www.nytimes.com/2006/08/30/world/europe/30iht-poland.2644508.html?_r=0

[171] Janusz Szczukowski, quoted in Olejarczyk, op. cit.

hefty fine and the confiscation of their ship.[172] With that the *Gustloff* has finally been left in peace. Lying on her port side, encrusted with sea-life and festooned with torn fishing nets, she is listed on Polish navigation charts simply as "Obstacle No. 73".

*

The total number killed when the *Wilhelm Gustloff* was torpedoed will never be known for sure. It is not even known precisely how many were aboard her when she sank. For a long time, the figure of 6,000 dead was given, but this has since been revised upward. It is now thought that, in the chaos of those dying days of the war, the ship's officers stopped registering passengers at 7,956, which – combined with the military personnel aboard, and the late-comers from the *Reval* – gave a

---

[172] Olejarczyk, op. cit.

provisional total aboard the *Gustloff* of around 10,500 – nearly five times the capacity for which the ship was designed. Subtracting the 1,252 who survived the wreck, leaves a death toll estimated at 9,250,[173] making it the deadliest single maritime sinking in history.

The story of the *Wilhelm Gustloff* is certainly a remarkable one. She was, in many ways, the flagship of Nazi Germany; she was the pride of the KdF fleet before the war, the most famous of its cruise liners. More than that, perhaps, one might describe the *Gustloff* as the Nazi *Titanic*; even as Hitler's *Titanic*. The *Titanic* has always been seen – rightly or wrongly – as in some way symbolic; a parable on human failings. For Goebbels, who oversaw the reworking of the story for propaganda purposes, the *Titanic* delivered a lesson on the cruel cynicism of

---

[173] Explained in Schön, op. cit., pp. 10-11.

Anglo-American capitalism; where ordinary lives could be risked for the sake of profit. In truth – away from the Nazi theatre screens – it represented the hubris of a generation who believed that their technological prowess could conquer nature; that they could create a liner that was unsinkable.

The *Wilhelm Gustloff* was similarly symbolic; her short 8-year life neatly mirrored that of her odious parent; Hitler's Reich. She was also the product of hubris; launched in 1937, in the period when the 'glamour' of the Third Reich was at its height, when the Nazi Party could seemingly do no wrong, when the future really did seem to belong to them – she was a symbol of a generation who believed that their political prowess and their *Volksgemeinschaft* could conquer the world. With the outbreak of war in 1939, the *Gustloff*'s service as a hospital ship appeared to typify the early optimism of the mobilized society; all united with one will to prosecute a victorious war. Then, laid up in Gotenhafen harbour – her diesel engines mothballed, her luxurious cabins given over to accommodate U-boatmen – she came to symbolise the harsh realities of the monumental struggle then getting under way.

With that, the *Wilhelm Gustloff* might have slipped from history, ending her days tethered uselessly to the quay as 'war booty'; a rusting relic of more peaceful times, and a reminder of the Third Reich's wicked vitality. But fate would not have it that way. Instead she was pressed into service once again; and once again she would symbolise Germany's wider fate. Venturing out into the hostile waters of the Baltic, critically overladen with refugees, she would become a symbol both of Germany's final abandonment of her eastern provinces, and ultimately of the cataclysmic collapse of Germany itself, dragging Europe with it into the abyss. The 9,000 or so who died aboard the *Gustloff* would be lost in a boundless ocean of wartime suffering.

The *Gustloff* is still there – by turns wished away, ignored, and now finally accepted. She still languishes in comparative obscurity. Most readers would scarcely imagine that hers was the worst maritime disaster in history – despite her death toll being nearly six times larger than that of the *Titanic*, and nearly twice as big as the next nearest contender. Where she is known about at all, she still arouses controversy; with some decrying her sinking as a war crime (it wasn't) and others crudely proclaiming that they had no sympathy for the victims – half of whom were children – because they were

Germans.[174] Seven decades after the event, can we not finally tell the sinking of the *Wilhelm Gustloff* as a human story, without the binary, tribal identities of the war having to intrude?

Whatever the answer to that, the *Gustloff*'s crumpled, barnacle-encrusted hull is now a symbol of Germany's *Vergangenheitsbewältigung*; its ongoing struggle to come to terms with its hideous past, and its hesitant efforts to incorporate the controversial aspect of German victimhood into the dominant narrative of collective guilt. Like the wreck itself, it is an issue that refuses to go away, and will be with us – just beneath the surface – for some considerable time to come.

---

[174] Both opinions were expressed in reply to my Twitter posting on the subject of the Gustloff in January 2016.

Acknowledgements

Even a short project such as this incurs a few debts along the way; not least to Richard Foreman and Endeavour Press for taking it on. Few know the wreck of the *Wilhelm Gustloff* as well as Tomasz Stachura, and our correspondence on the subject was as enjoyable as it was enlightening. Anastazja Pindor gave invaluable help with Polish sources on the *Gustloff* and Bill Niven deserves huge thanks for his generosity in sharing both his insights and a few relevant gems from his files.

Lastly, thanks must go to the late Heinz Schön, without whose tireless, and sometimes thankless, work researching, collating and archiving on the subject of the *Gustloff*, this book (and most others on the topic) would have been impossible.

For that reason, I humbly dedicate this book to him.

Author's Note

As ever, when one deals with the history of Central Europe, one runs the risk of offence or anachronism with the issue of place names. By way of explanation, throughout this book I have used place names that were current *at the time*; so using 'Danzig' for the Nazi period, but 'Gdańsk' after 1945.

Printed in Great Britain
by Amazon